THE MISSION

SRILA PRABHUPADA AND HIS DIVINE AGENTS

THE MISSION

SRILA PRABHUPADA AND HIS DIVINE AGENTS

Srila B. B. Bodhayan Goswami Maharaja

MANDALA

CONTENTS

PART TWO
DIVINE AGENTS

INTRODUCTION

The Supreme Lord Sri Krishna appeared in His most magnanimous mood, as Lord Chaitanya, to spread Divine Love without discrimination in terms of gender, caste, creed, nationality, etc. Lord Chaitanya's desire is that this Divine Love spreads to every town and village around the world. Lord Chaitanya manifested His pastimes in this world for 48 years. After His physical disappearance from this mortal world, the loving message of Sri Chaitanya Mahaprabhu was being purely preached by His spiritual descendants. However, after the departure of Srila Baladev Vidyabhushan Prabhu, many people, claiming to be followers of Sri Chaitanya Mahaprabhu, began to divert from the pure philosophy of Divine Love as propagated by Him. As a result, there appeared many groups of *apasampradaya* (bogus lineage). Some examples include *aula, baula, kartabhaja, neda, daravesa, sani sahajiya, sakhibheki, smarta, jata-gosani, ativadi, cudadhari* and *gauranga-nagari*[1]. Under the pretense of being the followers of Lord Chaitanya, they were in fact misrepresenting the philosophy only to serve their own interests and to fulfill their material sense enjoyment and desires.

The misrepresentation of Lord Chaitanya's teachings went on for many years. As we know from various scriptural sources, whenever spiritual principles are not being followed according to the scriptures, the Supreme Lord personally appears or sends His own representatives to establish pure spirituality again. In this way, Srila Saccidananda Bhaktivinoda Thakura appeared to re-establish proper spiritual principles in this

---

1 *Sri Chaitanya-charitamrita, Adi-lila*, 7.48

world. Srila Bhaktivinoda Thakura wrote many spiritual books which illuminate the path of Vaishnavism. In order to spread the Divine Love and Srila Bhaktivinoda Thakura's writing to the masses, the Supreme Lord sent another of His spiritual descendants into the family of Srila Bhaktivinoda Thakura. He was Srila Prabhupada Bhaktisiddhanta Saraswati Goswami Thakura (hereinafter referred to as 'Srila Prabhupada').

From the time of his birth in 1874, throughout his life, there were so many signs and events that indicated the divine nature of Srila Prabhupada. His unswerving dedication to his *bhajan* (spiritual practice) and exemplary manner in which he carried Lord Chaitanya's desire is unparalleled. His overwhelming love for the Lord was reciprocated, as, upon Srila Prabhupada expressing his concern regarding his inability to spread the loving message of Sri Krishna Chaitanya Mahaprabhu, the Lord and his *guru-varga* sent several outstanding individuals to Srila Prabhupada as his 'manpower' to assist.

Over a period of 18 years, between 1918 and 1936, Sriman Mahaprabhu sent severable remarkable, stalwart spiritual personalities (rays) to aid Srila Prabhupada in this mission. Lord Chaitanya's mission was successfully propagated by Srila Prabhupada Bhaktisiddhanta Saraswati Goswami Thakura. Srila Prabhupada's preaching mission was an exact replica of Lord Sri Krishna Chaitanya's mission. In fact, Srila Prabhupada was celebrated as the embodiment of Lord Chaitanya's preaching mission in this age of deception (*Kali-yuga*) Whoever follows Srila Prabhupada's footsteps will obviously reach Goloka Vrindavan, the abode of Sri Sri Radha Krishna.

This book aims to provide a small glimpse into the unquestionable greatness of Srila Prabhupada and his many rays (his disciples). It is a collection of the writings of various individuals in the Gaudiya Vaishnava community in conjunction with my humble contribution. I would like to express my heartfelt gratitude to all those who have contributed to the content in any way.

My humble prayer at the lotus feet of Srila Prabhupada is for him to kindly give me the strength to follow his last instruction: that everyone should be united under one shelter – the shelter of Srimati Radharani– and to spread Srila Rupa and Raghunath Goswami's message with great enthusiasm for the rest of my life. I also wish to serve his mission under the shelter of my spiritual master, His Divine Grace Srila Bhakti Pramode Puri Goswami Thakura, the founder of Sri Gopinath Gaudiya Math.

Trying to be a tiny particle at the lotus feet of my spiritual master. An unworthy servant of Lord Chaitanya's Mission,

B.B. Bodhayan
President, Sri Gopinath Gaudiya Math

श्री श्री ब्रजमण्डल-प

PART ONE

HISTORY

CHAPTER ONE

SPIRITUAL LINEAGE

Sri Krishna Chaitanya
Mahaprabhu

— 1486 to 1534 —

In 1486 A.D., the Supreme Lord Sri Krishna manifested the pastime of taking birth in Mayapur, Nadia, West Bengal in the form of Lord Chaitanya. Around the time of His birth, the social system of India was in turbulence. All the rulers were unnecessarily torturing the citizens, and the *brahmanas* were misusing their position and mistreating people of other castes.

During that period, Lord Chaitanya appeared to distribute pure love for the Supreme Lord Sri Sri Radha Krishna to one and all, without discrimination. He was the manifestation of divine love – *prema-purusottama*. He appeared to reveal to all mankind the means to realize their real identity, which surpasses the confines of race, color, creed, and caste, and to thus, bring an end to all types of discrimination and hate that may be held against one another. He wanted us to see everyone as eternal servants of the Lord and understand that we should respect everyone, and that the goal of life is to always fix our minds in the service of the Lord.

He also taught us that we should maintain our material duties towards our parents, children, husband, wife, neighbors and relatives without attachment. Alongside our material duties, we should practice spirituality instead of fighting one another in the name of religion and false prestige. In order to practice spirituality in this Age of Kali and to bring peace and harmony to society, He instructed us to chant the Hare Krishna *mana-mantra*:

Hare Krishna Hare Krishna
Krishna Krishna Hare Hare
Hare Rama Hare Rama
Rama Rama Hare Hare

He remained physically present on earth from 1486 to 1534. For the first twenty-four years, He performed His childhood pastimes, and as a young man, He lived as a householder. For the last twenty-four years of His manifest pastimes, He was in the renounced order (*sannyasa*).

In 1534, He returned to His spiritual abode through the pastime of disappearing from this world simultaneously from three different locations. He merged into the body of the Lord Jagannath deity in Jagannath Puri; He entered into the deity of Tota Gopinatha; and He disappeared from the vision of everyone while walking into the Mahodadhi Ocean at Jagannath Puri. These three occurrences miraculously took place in Jagannath Puri. Just as the Lord enters this world by His own sweet will, in the same way, He also mysteriously disappears from this world.

Srila Saccidananda
Bhaktivinoda Thakura

— 1838 to 1914 —

After Lord Chaitanya went back to His own abode in the spiritual world, the pure devotional practice established by Him, known as the Gaudiya Vaishnava tradition, began to gradually enter a phase of darkness and uncertainty. Many opportunists took on the garb of Vaishnavas but were preaching their own mental concoctions and deviated the general mass away from the path of surrender and pure love for the Divine Couple, Sri Sri Radha Krishna, as taught by Lord Chaitanya. Srila Bhaktivinoda Thakura revived the pure lineage of Gaudiya Vaishnavism in the 19th century. He was famously known as the seventh *goswami*. (Note: the famous six *goswamis* of Vrindavan were directly instructed by Sri Chaitanya Mahaprabhu to reveal the hidden truths of Sri Sri Radha Krishna, Their pastimes, places of pastimes and the rules and regulations to attain divine love.)

Srila Bhaktivinoda Thakura was born as Kedarnath Datta on 2 September 1838 and belonged to a wealthy *zamindar* (landlord) family from Birnagar, Ranaghat, West Bengal. His father, Sri Ananda Chandra Datta, and mother, Jaganmohini Devi, both were spiritually inclined. In his early years, he was exceptionally studious. In his university days, he associated with the intellectuals of the Bengali Renaissance. He studied numerous philosophical systems of both the East and the West and was also an accomplished poet. His career culminated in his post as District Magistrate, which was the highest post available to a native Indian under the rule of the British Raja.

In his 29th year, he became a dedicated follower of Sri Chaitanya Mahaprabhu, and very quickly established himself as a prominent and influential member of the Gaudiya Vaishnava community through his own example. Always thinking of how to present Mahaprabhu's teachings to a modern world, he authored over one hundred books in a variety of languages. He departed this mortal world on 23 June 1914 at his Calcutta residence, named Bhakti Bhavan, leaving his legacy behind for the service of Lord Chaitanya's mission.

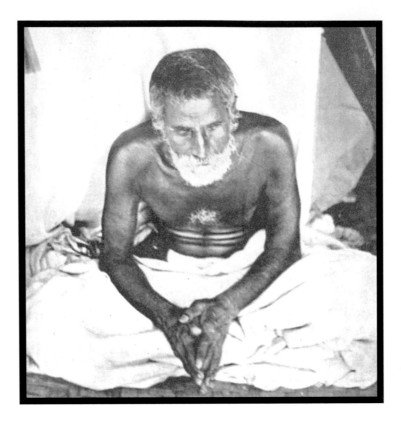

Srila Gaura Kishore Das
Babaji Maharaja

— 1838 to 1915 —

Sri Vamsi Das was the family name of Srila Gaura Kishore Das Babaji Maharaja. He was born in November 1838 in a simple mercantile family in a village called Vegyana near Tepakhola, which falls in the district of Faridpur. Faridpur is situated in present-day Bangladesh. At the age of thirty, after the physical demise of his wife, he found inspiration from being in the association of Srila Jagannath Das Babaji Maharaja to dedicate his life in following the Gaudiya Vaishnava tradition. He received initiation from Srila Nimai Chand Goswami, who was the descendant of Sri Advaita Acharya, in the lineage coming down from one of his sons, called Srila Krishna Mishra Prabhu. Later, he accepted the renounced order known as *babaji vesh* from Srila Bhagavat Das Babaji Maharaja.

In early 1900 A.D., Srila Gaura Kishore Das Babaji Maharaja accepted a disciple who would be his only disciple, called Sri Varshabhanavi-devi-dayita Das, who later became known as Srila Prabhupada Bhaktisiddhanta Saraswati Goswami Thakura, the founder president of the entire Gaudiya Math.

Srila Gaura Kishore Das Babaji Maharaja used to stay in Vrindavan Dham and Navadwip Dham. While he was in Navadwip Dham, every afternoon he visited Swananda Sukhada Kunja, where he would go to the residence of Saccidananda Srila Bhaktivinoda Thakura to listen to *harikatha* (*Srimad Bhagavatam* discourse). On 17 November 1915, in Navadwip Dham and on the most auspicious day of Utthana Ekadasi, Srila Gaura Kishore Das Babaji Maharaja's disappeared from this mortal world. According to *akinchan* Srila Krishnadas Babaji Maharaja's realization, Srila Babaji Maharaja is Vinoda Manjari in Krishna's eternal abode and pastimes.

CHAPTER TWO

A Short Biography of Srila Prabhupada

namo oṁ viṣṇu-pādāya kṛṣṇa-preṣṭhāya bhūtale
śrīmate bhaktisiddhānta-sarasvatīti nāmine

"I humbly offer my obeisance to *oṁ viṣṇu-pāda* Srila Bhaktisiddhanta Saraswati Thakura Prabhupada, who is most dear to Sri Krishna."

On Friday, 6 February 1874, in Jagannath Puri, at the home of the magistrate Sri Kedarnath Datta (widely known as Srila Bhaktivinoda Thakura), a blissful divine ray from the bejeweled eyes of Srimati Radharani appeared. To inform us of the baby's divinity, Srimati Radharani arranged that the baby boy was born with his umbilical cord wrapped around his body like a *brahmana* thread (*yagna upavita*). The father, Sri Kedarnath Datta, and mother, Srimati Bhagavati Devi, named the baby Bimala Prasad.

Several astrological scholars came to see the newborn baby. According to the time of his birth, the scholars predicted that Bimala Prasad would spread the glories of Lord Jagannath all over the world, as foretold by Vedavyasa in the *Padma Purana* – *hy utkale puruṣottamāt.* Sri Kedarnath Datta's whole family was blessed to see the baby, Bimala Prasad.

According to tradition, the baby was to consume grains for the first time during the *annaprashan* ceremony at the age of sixth months. The sixth-month ceremony took place during the most famous Jagannath Puri Ratha Yatra (chariot) festival, where hundreds of thousands of people had gathered. Miraculously, Lord Jagannath's chariot stopped in front of the home of Kedarnath. All endeavors by priests and devotees to pull or push Lord

Jagannath's chariot were in vain. Two days passed like this. On the third day, they were still unsuccessful in moving the chariot. That day, Bhagavati Devi was holding her six-month-old Bimala Prasad in her arms and looking at Lord Jagannath. As soon as Lord Jagannath saw Bimala Prasad, a garland miraculously fell from Lord Jagannath's neck. Lord Jagannath's priest took that garland and offered it to Bimala Prasad. As soon as this happened, Lord Jagannath's chariot began to move again. It seemed like Lord Jagannath wanted to greet his intimate devotee who would soon be spreading His glories.

Gradually, Bimala Prasad grew up and began performing significant activities. One day, Kedarnath Datta brought home ripe mangoes to offer to his deities. Bimala Prasad, out of his childish nature, took a ripe mango and bit into it. His father said, "First, we should offer everything to the Lord. If we eat anything without offering it, this will be considered stealing and is disrespectful to the Lord." As soon as Bimala Prasad heard this, he decided that for the rest of his life he would never eat ripe mangoes, a vow which he fulfilled. Since his childhood, Bimala Prasad displayed great determination. His example teaches us that we must also be determined in order to attain any goal.

By seven years of age, Bimala Prasad was initiated into the chanting of the Hare Krishna *mana-mantra* on *tulasi* beads (*harinama* – first initiation) by his father, Kedarnath Datta. He also received the Nrisimha *mantra*. He had completed listening to the entire *Chaitanya Shiksamrita* from his father by this age as well. Bimala Prasad was then initiated into the Kurma *mantra* and worship of the Kurma deity found during the excavation and construction of Kedarnath Datta's Calcutta residence, Bhakti Bhavan.

Bimala Prasad displayed astonishing educational talent. By the age of nine, he had memorized all 700 verses of the *Srimad Bhagavad Gita*. He began his education at an English-medium school in Ranaghat and then proceeded to Oriental Seminary in Calcutta. His razor-sharp intelligence and memory power were indescribable; he could remember verses and passages, verbatim, from any book that he read just once. He composed Sanskrit poetry since his childhood. An 11-year-old Bimala Prasad used to associate with leading Bengali Vaishnavas as part of the Vishva Vaishnava Raj Sabha, which was established by Kedarnath Datta. This association inspired Bimala Prasad to deeply study Vaishnava texts, which were part of his father's new Vaishnava Depository Library and printing press, located in the Bhakti Bhavan Calcutta residence.

By the age of 12, he was proofreading the articles, poetry, book reviews, etc. which were published as part of his father's monthly magazine, the *Sajjana-toshani*. At the age of 13, Bimala Prasad had entered the Vidyasagar College (known then as Calcutta Metropolitan Institution), where he gained a modern education. His studies included Sanskrit, mathematics and astrology, and due to his vast understanding and proficiency in astrology, he was given the title 'Siddhanta Saraswati'. His teachers were amazed by his high level of intelligence in every subject.

At the age of 18, Bimala Prasad was admitted into Sanskrit College, which was the prime institution for learning in Calcutta. There, he deeply studied the *Vedas* instead of studying mundane curriculum. Bimala Prasad always took great interest in studying his father's literary works, Narottama Thakura's *Prarthana* and *Prema-bhakti-candrika,* and other such works. Although he had studied extensive Sanskrit grammar texts such as

Siddhanta-kaumudi under the advice of scholars, he told his professors that life is meant for worshiping the Supreme Lord and not for the sole purpose of studying verb roots and grammar. Bimala Prasad wrote, "If I go on to study at the university, my family will inevitably harass me to get married. On the other hand, if I present myself as a useless fool, no one will try to interest me in that kind of life." He soon left Sanskrit College and decided to find a means of maintaining his livelihood with minimum effort whilst devoting maximum time for devotion to Krishna.

By the age of 21, Bimala Prasad became the secretary and historian of Bir Chandra Manikya, the king of Tripura, and later tutored the princes at the palace. At the age of 24, Siddhanta Saraswati opened the Saraswata Chatuspathi Sanskrit school at Bhakti Bhavan, wherein many important scholars came to study astrology. He also traveled to many places of pilgrimage from the north to the south of India together with his father. He deeply studied the teachings of Ramanujacharya and Madhvacharya and had books in the four South Indian languages brought to him. His father added the prefix "Bhakti" onto his name due to Bimala Prasad's deep interest in Vaishnava studies, making his name "Bhaktisiddhanta Saraswati".

Bimala Prasad was not an ordinary man. The following story is an example of this. Kedarnath Datta had eight sons and five daughters. His sons were Annada Prasad, Radhika Prasada, Viraja Prasad, Kamala Prasad, Bimala Prasad, Varada Prasad, Lalita Prasad, and Shailaja Prasad. His daughters were Soudamini Devi, Kadambini Devi, Krishna-vinodini Devi, Shyam-sarojini Devi, and Hari Pramodini. One time, Annada Prasad was seriously ill and no medical treatments, exorcisms, etc. were successful in curing him. Kedarnath Datta and Bhagavati Devi were searching for a solution. Suddenly,

Annada Prasad had a revelation in his heart that he was a devotee of the Ramanuja Sampradaya in his previous life. Annada Prasad told his father that, at that time, he had somehow committed an offense to Bimala Prasad and that was the reason for suffering now. Kedarnath Datta advised Annada Prasad to go and beg pardon from Bimala Prasad. As soon as Annada Prasad explained all this to Bimala Prasad, Bimala Prasad replied with due respect, "O, my elder brother, I don't know what offense you committed, but I forgive all of your offenses." After hearing Bimala Prasad's words, Annada Prasad was miraculously cured, and he physically passed away shortly thereafter.

In 1901, at the age of 27 and upon the order of his father, Bimala Prasad accepted *mahabhagavat* Gaura Kishore Das Babaji Maharaja as his *guru* in Godrumadvipa and was known as Varshabhanavi-devi-dayita Das thereafter. At the age of 31, Bimala Prasad began staying in Mayapur and took a vow to chant one billion (ten *crore*) holy names. He chanted a daily minimum of 300,000 names (192 rounds on a rosary of 108 beads), observed the vows of *chaturmasya*, such as eating boiled rice and lentils off the floor, and practiced complete austerity. During this vow, in 1914 Bhaktivinoda Thakura left this world, and in 1915 Gaura Kishore Das Babaji Maharaja followed. In a mood of great distress and separation, Varshabhanavi-devi-dayita Das (Bimala Prasad) thought he would give up the preaching mission as he had lost both of his spiritual shelters. He thought, instead, to devote the rest of his life solely to chanting the holy names.

One day, in the early morning hours, Varshabhanavi-devi-dayita Das had a vision in which Gaura Kishore Das Babaji, Bhaktivinoda Thakura, the six *goswamis* (Rupa, Sanatana, Raghunath Das, Raghunath Bhatta, Gopala Bhatta, and Jiva), Sri Chaitanya Mahaprabhu, Sri Nityananda Prabhu, Sri Advaita Acharya, Sri Gadadhar Pandit and Sri Srivasa Thakura all appeared and told him, "Bimala Prasad, give up your idea of spending the rest of your life in solitary chanting. You must spread the holy names." Bimala Prasad replied with his eyes full of tears, "How will I preach? You have all disappeared and I do not have any manpower to spread the divine love through the holy names." All of the divine personalities assured Bimala Prasad, "We will personally send you the required manpower and resources. Do not worry. Go and preach the message of divine love."

Thereafter, Bimala Prasad came back to his external senses and completed his vow of chanting one billion holy names. On the day of Gaura Purnima in 1918, at the age of 44, he accepted the vow of *tridandi-sannyasa* (commonly referred to as *sannyasa*) according to the rules and regulations he had learned from the *pandits* of the Ramanujacharya lineage. He established the Sri Chaitanya Math in Sridham Mayapur, Nadia as his first preaching center (also referred to as the Gaudiya Math). He was, thereafter, known as Bhaktisiddhanta Saraswati Goswami. In the same year, the society of Vaishnava scholars saw his determination and purity in carrying on the mission of Lord Chaitanya Mahaprabhu and bestowed upon him the title 'Prabhupada.' In short, people called him Srila Prabhupada.

Gradually, many intellectual giants from reputed families joined Srila Prabhupada's mission, such as Kunjabihari Vidyabhushan (Bhakti Vilas Tirtha Goswami), Jagadish Bhakti Pradip (Bhakti Pradip Tirtha Goswami), Paramananda Vidyaratna, Ananta Vasudeva, Pranavananda (Bhakti Pramode Puri Goswami), Sundarananda Vidyavinode, Hayagriva (Bhakti Dayita Madhava Goswami), Ramendra Sundar (Bhakti Rakshak Sridhar Goswami), Vinode Da (Bhakti Prajnan Keshava Goswami), Nayanabhirama (Bhakti Vivek Bharati Goswami), Patitapavana (Bhakti Keval Audulomi Goswami), Nandasunu (Bhakti Hridaya Bon Goswami), Aprakrita Bhakti Saranga (Bhakti Saranga Goswami), Abhay Charanaravinda (Bhaktivedanta Swami Goswami) and so on. In this manner, Srila Prabhupada began his vast preaching efforts both nationally and internationally. With the assistance of his associates, Srila Prabhupada preached all over India.

In 1933, he sent Bhakti Pradip Tirtha Goswami Maharaja, Bhakti Hridaya Bon Goswami Maharaja, Bhakti Saranga Goswami Maharaja and Samvidananda Prabhu to Europe as the first preachers of Lord Chaitanya's message in the West. Srila Prabhupada also gave the order to Abhay Charanaravinda Prabhu (later known as Bhaktivedanta Swami Goswami Maharaja)

to preach Lord Chaitanya's message in the English language. For eighteen years from 1918 to 1936, Srila Prabhupada massively spread Lord Chaitanya's loving mission and established sixty-four preaching centers across India, Europe and Southeast Asia.

I heard from my spiritual master, Srila Bhakti Pramode Puri Goswami Maharaja, how Srila Prabhupada would eloquently answer any queries that were posed to him in a strikingly clear manner. If a geography, history or mathematics professor came to ask any questions, he would answer accordingly, citing examples from each subject matter. Srila Prabhupada was known as a living universal encyclopedia.

I also heard how Srila Prabhupada never spent even a moment away from the Lord's services. Even during his morning walks, Srila Prabhupada used to give dictation to three different people on three different topics, simultaneously. During his physical presence, Srila Prabhupada's associates were able to publish daily, weekly, fortnightly and monthly newsletters and magazines. They were also able to print and publish many books, such as Srila Prabhupada's commentary on the *Chaitanya-Bhagavat,* called the *Gaudiya-bhasya,* Srila Prabhupada's commentary on the *Chaitanya-charitamrita,* called the *Anu-bhasya,* the *Srimad Bhagavatam,* all Bhaktivinoda Thakura's books, many of the *goswamis'* literatures and so on. Nowadays, many of the books published by various Gaudiya Maths are all compiled mainly based on Srila Prabhupada's writings and dictations.

Srila Prabhupada's determination was very attractive. My spiritual master would often recount the incident of the International Religious Conference in Calcutta, where Srila Prabhupada instructed Sarvesvara Brahmachari (Srila Bhakti Vichar Jajabar Goswami Maharaja) to present the philosophy of the Gaudiya

Math and did not waiver from this decision. The incident is described in detail in Chapter 7.3.

Srila Prabhupada used to teach everyone through example. I would like to narrate one such incident. We know from the scriptures that *mahaprasad* is considered to be completely pure, even if touched by the mouth of a dog. A disciple of Srila Prabhupada, Sri Atul Chandra Bandopadhyay (later known as Srila Bhakti Saranga Goswami Maharaja), was very skilled in collecting funds for the temple, in preaching and in a variety of temple-related services. One day, he had gone out to preach and returned to the temple late. *Prasadam* had long been served and was finished in the kitchen. Not having anything to eat, he approached the person in charge of the kitchen (*bhandari*) and began yelling at him for having not saved any *prasadam* for him. Srila Prabhupada was chanting in his room after taking *prasadam* when he heard Atul Chandra yelling. He came out of his room and called him over. Srila Prabhupada said, "Come with me." Then, Srila Prabhupada took Atul Chandra to the garbage site where all the *prasadam* remnants and used leaf plates were thrown. There was a group of dogs eating the leftover remnants at that garbage site. Srila Prabhupada shooed away all the dogs, knelt, picked up a few grains of rice and ate them. He said to Atul Chandra, "This is *mahaprasad*." Through this incident, Srila Prabhupada taught us about the inconceivable value of *mahaprasad*.

Once, at an All-India Conference of Panditas at Midnapore, presided over by Pandita Vishvambhara-anandadeva Goswami, Srila Prabhupada, taking the place of Bhaktivinoda Thakura, who was ill at the time, lectured to an astounded audience on the comparative position of a *brahmana* and a Vaishnava. After the discourse all the people came forward to offer him respect and touch his lotus feet. The president of the conference

called him the other self of Sri Sukadeva Goswami. The
lecture was subsequently published as a book in Bengali.

The following incident is one that my spiritual master
used to narrate. A few days before Srila Prabhupada's
departure, Kunja Babu and Srila Bhakti Rakshak
Sridhar Dev Goswami were present in Prabhupada's
room. Suddenly, Srila Prabhupada ordered Srila Sridhar
Goswami Maharaja to sing *Sri Rupa Manjari Pada*. Just
as Srila Sridhar Goswami Maharaja was about to sing,
Kunja Babu said, "Wait. I will call Pranava. He has a
sweet voice." Upon hearing Kunja Babu's call for him,
Sripad Pranavananda entered Srila Prabhupada's room
and began to sing (as he thought it was Prabhupada's
desire for him to sing). Just as he started singing,
Prabhupada interjected and said, "I said that Sridhar
Maharaja should sing this song, so let him sing first."
Thereafter, Srila Sridhar Maharaja sang the song *Sri*

Rupa Manjari Pada. Immediately after hearing this song, Srila Prabhupada said, "Now, Pranava, sing *Hari He Doyal Mora Jaya Radhanath.* Then, Sripad Pranavananda sang the song. This example shows how Srila Prabhupada used to respect everyone while simultaneously ensuring that whatever he instructed was followed. Whoever follows Srila Prabhupada's instructions will undoubtedly attain the supreme spiritual destination.

At 05:30 on 1 January 1937, we lost the physical presence of this gem as Srila Prabhupada departed from this world. All the clocks inside the Bag Bazar Gaudiya Math premises miraculously stopped at the exact moment of his departure, and it was as if the whole world became filled with inconceivable darkness.

Srila Prabhupada's entire life was filled with valuable lessons for us. By his own example, he showed how to be determined and progress in our spiritual practice with our best endeavor. By our following in his footsteps, the Lord will definitely accept our service and deliver us from this miserable world. Srila Prabhupada's legacy is the bright beacon of our devotional life. If anyone wholeheartedly follows Srila Prabhupada's exemplary character, that person will most certainly be freed from material entanglement and gradually progress towards achieving divine love for Sri Sri Radha Govinda, which will qualify him to go to our eternal home, Goloka Vrindavan. In this way, we will become eternally peaceful and blissful.

CHAPTER THREE

THE TRUE MEANING OF SRILA PRABHUPADA

Srila Bhaktisiddhanta Saraswati Goswami Thakura was honored with the title 'Prabhupada' by several Vaishnava scholars when he completed chanting one billion holy names. The scholars glorified him, saying, "You are the embodiment of Lord Chaitanya's preaching mission in this age of deception (*Kali-yuga*). It is extremely rare to find a person who is following Lord Chaitanya's order – first deserve then desire. You completed one billion names in 10 years, and also you are a live Vaishnava encyclopedia for us. We would like to give you a title – Srila Prabhupada. From today, instead of using your *sannyasa* name, everyone should call you with the title Srila Prabhupada."

The word 'Prabhupada' can be divided into two parts. The first part is *prabhu*, which means 'Lord', and the second part is *pada*, which means 'feet'. In Vaishnava tradition, to honor and glorify the Lord's feet, we use the word 'lotus' as a decorative description to describe the Lord's feet (lotus feet).

People from various groups use the word *prabhu* to refer to the object of their faith. Amongst Gaudiya-Vaishnava devotees, the use of *prabhu* indicates Sri Krishna Chaitanya Mahaprabhu, who according to Gaudiya Vaishnava scriptures is Lord Krishna Himself. He was known by different names: Nimai, Vishwambhar, Gauranga and many others.

In this age of quarrel, hypocrisy, ignorance and darkness, which we call *Kali-yuga*, Sri Krishna Chaitanya Mahaprabhu took a vow of renunciation in order to teach people how to surrender to the lotus feet of Krishna and receive His divine love in this age of *Kali*.

This vow of renunciation is called *tridandi-sannyasa*. Here *tridandi* means 'three' and refers to the body, mind and speech. *Sannyasa* means one who is fully removed from material attachments and is fully surrendered in body, mind and speech to the service of the Divine Couple, Sri Sri Radha-Krishna. After taking *sannyasa*, Nimai, or Vishwambhar as he was known, was named Sri Krishna Chaitanya. Gaudiya Vaishnava devotees use another decorative word, 'Mahaprabhu', after His name to glorify Him. *Maha* means great. In order to respect the *sannyasa* name of their Lord, He was called Sri Krishna Chaitanya Mahaprabhu.

Lord Ramachandra is the incarnation of honor (*maryāda-puruṣottama*), and Lord Krishna is the incarnation of pastimes (*līlā-puruṣottama*). To the Gaudiya Vaishnavas, Sri Krishna Chaitanya Mahaprabhu is the incarnation of divine love (*prema-puruṣottama*). Gaudiya Vaishnavas' object of faith is Sri Krishna Chaitanya Mahaprabhu. Thus, for Gaudiya Vaishnava devotees, the word 'Prabhupada' glorifies the lotus feet of Sri Krishna Chaitanya Mahaprabhu.

The inner meaning of 'Prabhupada' for Gaudiya Vaishnava devotees exemplifies the manner by which the loving message of Sri Krishna Chaitanya Mahaprabhu is carried. Thus, 'Prabhupada' is one who is fully surrendered to spreading the loving message of Mahaprabhu with integrity.

Devotees of Gaudiya Vaishnavism accept their spiritual master as one who carries, in an exemplary manner, the loving message of Sri Krishna Chaitanya Mahaprabhu. Therefore, devotees in most branches of the lineage use the word 'Prabhupada' with the names of the following spiritual masters:

1. His Divine Grace Srila Rupa Goswami Prabhupada
2. His Divine Grace Srila Sanatana Goswami Prabhupada
3. His Divine Grace Srila Jiva Goswami Prabhupada
4. His Divine Grace
   Srila Raghunath Bhatta Goswami Prabhupada

5. His Divine Grace
   Srila Gopala Bhatta Goswami Prabhupada
6. His Divine Grace
   Srila Raghunath Das Goswami Prabhupada
7. His Divine Grace
   Srila Lokanatha Das Goswami Prabhupada
8. His Divine Grace
   Srila Krishnadasa Kaviraja Goswami Prabhupada
9. His Divine Grace
   Srila Bhaktivinoda Thakura Prabhupada and
10. His Divine Grace Srila Bhaktisiddhanta Saraswati
    Goswami Thakura Prabhupada.

In fact, all pure devotees who carry the loving message of Sri Krishna Chaitanya Mahaprabhu with integrity in the Gaudiya-Vaishnava tradition are eligible to use the title 'Prabhupada' with their names.

Out of humility, though, and in order to maintain special respect for their spiritual master, His Divine Grace Srila Bhaktisiddhanta Saraswati Goswami Thakura Prabhupada, most of his disciples did not allow anyone to address them with the title 'Prabhupada'. One exceptional and special case was His Divine Grace Srila Bhaktivedanta Swami Maharaja, founded the International Society for Krishna-Consciousness, ISKCON. He permitted his disciples to use the title 'Prabhupada' for him.

CHAPTER FOUR

DISCUSSIONS WITH
SRILA PRABHUPADA

This chapter narrates the interactions between two prominent individuals in society and Srila Prabhupada and gives a small glimpse into Srila Prabhupada's effective manner of conveying his message.

Netaji Subhash Chandra Bose

In 1930, Netaji Subhash Chandra Bose along with some of his famous associates came to visit Srila Prabhupada at Calcutta's Bag Bazar Gaudiya Math. Below is an excerpt of their conversation:

Netaji: I am bound by my determination to free our motherland from the colonization of the British. I have given the slogan "Give me your blood. I will give you freedom" to the whole nation. Now, I have come to know that many youths have taken shelter at your divine feet. Please tell some of them to join my movement so that they can take part in the fight for independence.

Prabhupada: Have you read the *Srimad Bhagavad Gita*?

Netaji: Yes, I have read it.

Prabhupada: In that case, you must certainly remember this verse from the *Gita*: *yaṁ yaṁ vāpi smaran bhāvaṁ tyajaty ante kalevaram taṁ tam evaiti kaunteya sadā tad-bhāva-bhāvitaḥ* – "O, son of Kunti devi, Kaunteya, one attains whatever he thinks of at the time of death and will be constantly absorbed in that mood."

Netaji: Yes, I remember that verse.

Prabhupada: In that case, you must certainly believe in reincarnation?

Netaji: Of course I believe in it. Is there any Hindu who does not believe in reincarnation?

Prabhupada: If in the course of circumstances, you die today and then take your next birth in England, then would you still be fighting for the independence of India, or would you be trying to protect your own country's control over India?

Netaji: I understand your logic. However, at this moment, it is fitting to think about independence for our nation.

Prabhupada: You are worried about all that is but impermanent and material, that is, material independence for our nation, thinking that we are Indians. However, the designation of being Indian is itself a material one. My worry is for humanity at large – how humanity can be freed from the bondage of material illusion. In actuality, I do not think just for humans, but rather for all living entities – how can they become free from material bondage? This is my mindset.

Netaji: I have never before heard such an eloquent explanation of the *Bhagavad Gita*. However, I just fear that our nation's independence movement does not get negatively affected.

After speaking these words, Netaji did not make any more requests from Srila Prabhupada and silently left.

Pandit Sriyukta
Madan Mohan Malaviya

On Friday, 17 April 1925 (Bangabda 4th Vaishakh 1331), Pandit Sriyukta Madan Mohan Malaviya came to meet Srila Prabhupada along with some other renowned scholars including Piyushkanti, who was the meritorious son of the famous Sishir Kumar Ghosh, and Sri Jiva Nyaytirtha, MA, who was the son of the late Pandit Sriyukta Panchanan Tarkaratna Mahashay.

Upon seeing Prabhupada, Pandit Malaviya said with great enthusiasm, "Today I have become fortunate. Today I truly have seen a great spiritual personality."

Panditji and Srila Prabhupada discussed the concept of *brahmanas* by quality. Prabhupada discussed the concept of Vajasaneya and Ekayanasakhi Vaishnava *brahmanas* from the 1000-year-old book *Agama Pramanya* of Sri Yamunacharya (the *guru* of the *guru* of Sri Ramanujacharya). He explained various Vedic evidences showing that *vaishnava-dharma* is *sanatana-dharma* and *suddha-bhakti* is the soul's true function (*atma-vrtti*).

Hearing these topics from Srila Prabhupada, Pandit Malaviya said, "It is necessary that these words of yours be preached in every village of Bengal, every home, throughout India and the world. Due to the famine in the preaching of *hari-bhakti* at present, the country is going toward the path of *adharma* and *apadharma* (unrighteousness). Thus, it is the right time to preach about devotion to Hari."

Srila Prabhupada replied to Pandit Malaviya saying, "By preaching *shraddha* and pure devotion, we are not going to get more votes from this world. I have heard you give classes on the *Srimad Bhagavat*. Therefore, you know for sure that the feature of *bhagavat dharma* is that

the Supreme Truth, which is free of impurity, Bhagavan
Sri Krishna, is served through pure devotion. Cultivating
other desires, *nitya-naimittika karma, nirbheda-brahma-jnana,
astanga-yoga, raja-yoga, vrata, tapasya* and false *vairagya* are
not considered to be pure devotion. *Srimad Bhagavat*
has said that all of these deal with the body. The pure,
constitutional, causeless, unhindered function of the
atma is *bhagavad-bhakti*. Vedic *pancopasana* (worship of five
gods) is not *suddha-bhakti*. This is because in *pancopasana*
the eternality of *bhakti* and Bhagavan is not accepted.
Accepting a temporary form of God just for achieving
some sense gratification or liberation is not *suddha-
bhakti*." In regard to this, Srila Prabhupada explained
the differences, unity, features, and attractiveness of

the Shankara, Ramanuja, Madhva and Mahaprabhu philosophies.

While hearing these explanations about the *Bhagavat* from Srila Prabhupada, Pandit Malaviya recited many verses from the *Bhagavat* supporting his words and spoke, "You have swum in the ocean of nectarine mellows of the *Bhagavat* and have become heavy. Thus, your fearlessness as a *guru* and *acharya* is exemplary to us. Spread this nectar to one and all through your behavior and by distributing the drops of the nectar to your disciples. There is no difference between genuine *brahmanya-dharma, vaidika-dharma* and *vaishnava-dharma*. If one becomes a true *brahmana*, then he can become a Vaishnava."

With great enthusiasm, Panditji said, "Please tell me when you will give me thousands of *brahmana* devotees; tell me when I shall get them from you."

Seeing the work of the Sri Gaudiya Math, and the exemplary behavior and character of the Math's *sannyasis* and *brahmacharis*, Panditji said, "I would like to see many, materially detached *brahmacharis* from you who can preach *bhakti* from door to door from sun-rise to sun-set."

When Panditji saw the deity of Sriman Mahaprabhu, he asked, "Why does this deity have His hands lifted upwards?" Prabhupada replied, "This is significant of Sriman Mahaprabhu preaching *harinama*." Panditji became especially pleased upon hearing this and expressed his congratulations to Prabhupada while asking for permission to leave. When it was time to leave, Sri Jiva Nyayatirtha said, "We will also join with you soon."

This meeting was printed in the *Amrta Bajar Patrika* on 18 April 1925 and in the daily *Forward* on 24 April 1925.

CHAPTER FIVE

VYASA PUJA
DISCOURSES

*This chapter provides the essence of two
discourses that Srila Prabhupada gave
during his Vyasa Puja Festivals.*

First Vyasa Puja

Most worshipful Sri Srila Prabhupada's 50th appearance day was on Sunday 12th Phalgun 1330, 24 February 1924, Maghi Krishna-pancami. The disciples of Srila Prabhupada celebrated his Vyasa Puja, or worship of the spiritual master, for the first time at Sri Gaudiya Math located at No. 1 Ultadingi Junction in Calcutta.

The appearance day of the *guru* is celebrated with great reverence and honour as Sri Vyasa Puja or Sri Guru Puja. For the benefit of us ignorant souls, Srila Prabhupada delivered a discourse on the essence and glories of Vyasa Puja so that we understand its true significance. Following below is a synopsis of his discourse.

Srila Krishnadasa Kaviraja Goswami has stated multiple times in *Sri Chaitanya-charitamrita* that Srila Vrindavan Das Thakura has described the pastimes of Sri Chaitanya in *Sri Chaitanya Bhagavat* just as Sri Krishna Dvaipayana Vyasa has described the pastimes of Sri Krishna in *Srimad Bhagavat.*

*kṛṣṇa-līlā bhāgavate kahe vedavyāsa
caitanya-līlāra vyāsa – vṛndāvana dāsa*

(*Sri Chaitanya-charitamrita, Adi-lila,* 8.34)

That Srila Vrindavan Das Thakura has written that the appearance day of Sri Sriman Mahaprabhu, who is non-different from Svayam Bhagavan Vrajendranandana, is on Phalguni Paurnamasi and that the appearance day of Sri Sri Nityananda Prabhu, who is non-different from Sriman Mahaprabhu and who is the form of Sri Bhagavan Baladeva, is on Maghi Sukla Trayodasi. Both of these days are the personifications of devotion and are full of auspiciousness. All auspicious times are present within them. Both of these days give birth to devotion as they are the days of Sri Madhava. By celebrating the Lords on these days, one obtains devotion to Krishna and inadvertently, the bondage of lack of knowledge (*avidyā*) is destroyed. Just as the appearance day of Sri Bhagavan is pure, in the same way, His dear devotees' appearance days are pure:

eteke e dui tithi karile sevana
kṛṣṇa-bhakti haya khaṇḍe avidyā-bandhana

īśvarera janma-tithi ye-hena pavitra
vaiṣṇavera sei mata tithira caritra

(*Sri Chaitanya Bhagavat, Adi-lila,* 3.47-48)

Most worshipful Srila Prabhupada has written in his *Gaudiya Bhasya,* "By serving these two days, namely Maghi Sukla Trayodasi and Phalguni Purnima, the bondage of ignorance is destroyed and the tendency to serve Krishna is born. These days are days for performing austerities in the name of the appearance of the Lords (*jayanti-vrata*) or are also known as the appearance days of God (*avirbhava-divasa*). These days are served by fasting and celebrating on the days. The appearance days of the Lord's devotees are just as pure as the appearance days of God. Celebrations should definitely take place on such days."

Vyasa is the person who divided the *Vedas*, Sri Krishna Dvaipayana Vyasa. Another meaning of the word *vyasa* is division, distribution or expansion. Sri Bhagavan Vedavyasa mercifully divided the *Vedas* into four parts and composed the *Itihasas* and *Puranas* (histories) to clarify the *Vedas*. The *Itihasas* and *Puranas* are known as the fifth *Veda*. It is stated in the *Mahabharata*: *itihāsa-purāṇābhyāṁ vedāṁśam upabṛṁhayet*. The meaning of the *Vedas* has been made clear through the *Mahabharata, Itihasas* and *Puranas*. Vedavyasa expanded the meaning of the *Vedas*, made the meaning clear, distributed the meaning of the *Vedas* everywhere and is thus known as Vedavyasa. Sri Gurudeva is known to be non-different from Sri Vyasa because he also always relishes the nectar of the topics related to Sri Krishna and distributes those topics. The *Vayu Purana* states:

ācinoti yaḥ śāstrārtham ācāre sthāpayaty api
svayam ācarate yasmād ācāryas tena kīrtitaḥ

"One who adeptly compiles the scriptural conclusions, practices them and establishes those teachings is known as an *acharya*, as he practices the instructions in his own behavior and is a knower of the truth."

Therefore, an *acharya's* work is to practice and preach the conclusions of pure devotion. For this reason, the spiritual master is considered to be non-different from Sri Vyasa and his worship is performed on the Sri Vyasa Puja.

Most worshipful Srila Prabhupada has also made known, "Another name for Sri Vyasa Puja is worship of the lotus feet of Sri Guru Pada-padma (*padya-arpana*) or fulfillment of the desire of Sri Gurudeva, which is excellent performance of service to Bhagavan."

Thakura Narottama offers prayers to the lotus feet of Sri Rupa Goswami, considering him to be the one who fulfils the desires of Mahaprabhu as follows:

śrī-rūpa-mañjarī-pada, sei mora sampada,
sei mora bhajana-pūjana
sei mora prāṇa-dhana, sei mora ābharaṇa,
sei mora jīvanera jīvana

sei mora rasa-nidhi, sei mora vāñchā-siddhi,
sei mora vedera dharama
sei vrata, sei tapa, sei mora mantra-japa,
sei mora dharama-karama

"Sri Rupa Manjari's lotus feet are my treasure. They are my spiritual service and worship. They are the treasure of my very life. They are my ornaments, and they are the life of my life. They are the ocean of devotional mellows for me, and they are the perfection of my desires. They are my Vedic *dharma,* and they are my austerities and penances. They are my *mantra* chanting and they are my *dharma* and *karma.*"

Through various *kirtans,* the example of Sri Vyasa Puja has been highlighted through the worship of the lotus feet of Sri Sri Rupa. Most worshipful Srila Prabhupada has given us the *bhagavata-guru-parampara* following in the footsteps of Sri Rupa (*rupanuga*) and has said, "Our highest goal is to become the dust of the lotus feet of the followers of Sri Rupa. Our eternal constitutional position, birth after birth, is in being the dust of the lotus feet of Sri Rupa Prabhu. That is everything for us. The spiritual line of Bhaktivinoda will never be stopped. Become committed with even more enthusiasm to preaching the desire of Bhaktivinoda. Following one-pointedly in the footsteps of the followers of Sri Rupa, preach the message of Sri Rupa and Raghunath with utmost enthusiasm and fearlessness."

Through these words and more, Srila Prabhupada has clearly highlighted that Sri Vyasa Puja is to be celebrated by becoming committed to serving and fulfilling the desires of the followers of Sri Rupa. Srila Krishnadasa Kaviraja Goswami has written at the end of every chapter of his *Sri Chaitanya-charitamrita* – *śrī rūpa-raghunātha-pade yāra āśa caitanya-caritāmṛta kahe kṛṣṇadāsa*. Krishnadasa, whose desire is at the feet of Sri Rupa and Raghunath, speaks the nectarine stories of Chaitanya. Signing each chapter with his name in this manner, he has showed us how to follow in the footsteps of Sri Rupa and Raghunath. Sri Sanatana is the *acharya* of *sambandha-tattva*. Sri Rupa is the *acharya* of *abhidheya-tattva*. Sri Raghunath is the *acharya* of *prayojana-tattva*. In the *Sri Chaitanya-charitamrita*, Sri Vrajendranandana, who is the very life of Sri Radha, is He with whom relationship is to be established (*sambandha*). The means to achieving the goal is devotion to Krishna (*abhidheya*). The way in which Sri Radha has loved Krishna is the goal (*prayojana*). This has been made known. The teaching of Sri Rupa, Sanatana and Raghunath along with the conversation between Sriman Mahaprabhu and Ray Ramananda are included in that which Sri Srila Prabhupada calls as the words of Sri Rupa and Raghunath (*Sri Sri Rupa Raghunath Katha*). Therefore, serving those words is the fulfillment of the desire of Sri Guru Pada-padma. Completely committing oneself to serving the desire of Sri Guru Pada-padma, who is non-different from Sri Rupa Raghunath, is the actual worship of Sri Vyasa or Sri Guru Pada-padma (*Sri Vyasa Puja*). Simply performing external worship without internally offering oneself completely to fulfilling the desire and service of Sri Gurudeva is not considered as a true Vyasa Puja.

Sri Bhagavan Nityananda Prabhu first offered the Vyasa Puja flower garland on Sri Mahaprabhu's neck in the courtyard of Srivas Thakura, which is non-different from the *Rasa-sthali*, and in this way, showed the way in which Sri Vyasa Puja is to be performed. Sri Mahaprabhu is Krishna accompanied by *anga* (Sri Nityananda, Advaita), *upāṅga* (*śrīvāsādi bhakta-vṛnda*), *astra* (Sri Harinama), *parsada* (Sri Gadadhar Pandit, Svarupa Damodara, Raya Ramananda, etc.). Despite that, He accepts the mood of a devotee and displays the example of singing the names of Krishna with his form of golden complexion (*Gaura*). The worship of Sankritana-natha Gaurahari is to be done: *sei ta' sumedhā āra kali-hata jana samkīrtana-yajñe tānre kare ārādhana*. Those are the intelligent ones who perform the sacrifice of chanting the holy names and worship in this manner; the rest are people afflicted by the age of *Kali*. In accordance with this line of thought and worship as performed by intelligent persons, those who worship the spiritual master who fulfils the desires of Sri Chaitanya are showing the actual signs of intelligence. The Vyasa Puja performed by such people is actually successful. Most worshipful Srila Prabhupada established the practice of Vyasa Puja in this manner and taught us the true meaning of Vyasa Puja.

Last Vyasa Puja

Srila Prabhupada's last Vyasa Puja festival was held in 1936. During this time, Srila Prabhupada gave discourses over a five-day period. The available content from these discourses is provided here. Very limited content was available from Day 4, and therefore that day's teachings are incoherent. Please excuse this.

Day 1
12 February 1936

The essence of Sri Srila Prabhupada's teachings:

The system of Sri Vyasa Puja has been present since ancient times and there are certainly *mantras* for *Sri Vyasa Puja*. We seek the compassion of Sri Vyasadeva, the form of the original *guru*, who preached the message of the fifth goal of life (*pancam-purusartha*) through His composition of the *Srimad Bhagavatam*. He used to perform the worship of Purushottam and continues the worship at present. He is a portion of Sri Bhagavan and is considered an incarnation of the energy of the Lord (*saktyavesa avatara*). Everyone worships Him as the spiritual master (*guru*). The spiritual masters (*guru-pada-padmas*) are situated on the seat of Sri Vyasadeva. The servants worship the spiritual masters on the day of Sri Vyasa Puja.

Sri Chaitanya Mahaprabhu told Sri Nityananda Prabhu to perform the first Vyasa Puja during His advent. In accordance with that, Sri Nityananda told Srivasa Pandit to make the arrangements for the worship at Srivas Pandit's residence. When Srivas Pandit gave a garland to Sri Nityananda for garlanding Sri Vyasadeva, Nityananda said, "Yes. Yes," and waited for some time; when Mahaprabhu arrived, Nityananda garlanded

Mahaprabhu with that garland, Sri Nityananda Prabhu garlanded Him in the sense of Mahaprabhu being the spiritual master of the entire world (*jagad-guru*). Sri Vyasadeva has written at the beginning of the *Srimad Bhagavatam*:

janmādy asya yato 'nvayād itarataś cārtheṣv abhijñaḥ svarāṭ
tene brahma hṛdā ya ādi-kavaye muhyanti yat sūrayaḥ
tejo-vāri-mṛdāṁ yathā vinimayo yatra tri-sargo 'mṛṣā
dhāmnā svena sadā nirasta-kuhakaṁ satyaṁ paraṁ dhīmahi

> "In this context, *dhīmahi* is plural. We all, together, meditate on the non-dual supreme controller (*advaya-jñāna parameśvara vastu*). The work of creation, existence and destruction of this world, in forward sequence, and in reverse, is all carried out by the Supreme controller (*parameśvara*). The Supreme controller is omniscient in all respects regarding all the workings of the world. Knowledge which is perfect in and of itself rests in that Supreme controller. He inspired the intellect of the original poet, Brahma, and manifested the truth through him. Indra and the other gods become overcome with illusion when faced with the truth of that Supreme controller. Just as fire, water and earth seem to truly transform into one another, similarly, the modes of nature, namely goodness, passion and ignorance, seem to be truly present in the Supreme controller although in reality, it is impossible for the material modes and functions to be present within that Supreme Truth. We all meditate upon that Supreme non-dual Truth, the Supreme controller, who is totally free of deception."

Sri Guru-pada-padma Sri Vyasadeva teaches to meditate on that Supreme controller.

kṛte yad dhyāyato viṣṇuṁ tretāyāṁ yajato makhaiḥ
dvāpare paricaryāyāṁ kalau tad dhari-kīrtanāt

"In the *Satya-yuga*, the means to attain the Supreme was through meditation. In the *Treta-yuga*, the means to attain the Supreme was through sacrifice. In the *Dvapara-yuga*, the means to attain the Supreme was through deity worship, and in the *Kali-yuga*, the means to attain the Supreme is through singing the Holy Names."

Sri Sri Gaura Nitai preached the greatness of this congregational chanting of the Holy Names. Sri Nityananda Prabhu placed the garland on Sriman Mahaprabhu's neck. Sri Nityananda and Sriman Mahaprabhu were present in the courtyard of Srivasa Pandit. Srivasa and the other devotees are our spiritual masters. We will perform the Sri Vyasa Puja by following their example. Let us offer garlands to Them.

Day 2
13 February 1936

From the evening onwards, Srila Prabhupada spent two hours explaining the main *shlokas*, namely,

śrī-caitanya-mano-'bhīṣṭaṁ sthāpitaṁ yena bhū-tale
svayaṁ rūpaḥ kadā mahyaṁ dadāti sva-padāntikam

rādhā kṛṣṇa-praṇaya-vikṛtir hlādinī śaktir asmād
ekātmānāv api bhuvi purā deha-bhedaṁ gatau tau
caitanyākhyaṁ prakaṭam adhunā tad-dvayaṁ caikyam āptaṁ
rādhā-bhāva-dyuti-suvalitaṁ naumi kṛṣṇa-svarūpam

śrī-rādhāyāḥ praṇaya-mahimā kīdṛśo vānayaivā-
svādyo yenādbhuta-madhurimā kīdṛśo vā madīyaḥ
saukhyaṁ cāsyā mad-anubhavataḥ kīdṛśaṁ veti lobhāt
tad-bhāvāḍhyaḥ samajani śacī-garbha-sindhau harīnduḥ

The summary essence is as follows: Firstly, Sri Chaitanya is the non-dual Supreme Truth. He is present in two bodies as Sri Radha Govinda for the purpose of relishing the nectar of pastimes. Then again, in order to make known the love of Sri Radhika, Sri Chaitanya Himself, being Krishna internally, while taking upon the molten golden complexion of Sri Radhika externally, appeared in the material world. In describing the main reason for Mahaprabhu's appearance, the verse *śrī-rādhāyāḥ praṇaya-mahimā* has been quoted. The eight main heroines, namely *abhisarika, vasakasajja, utkanthita, khandita, vipralabdha, kalahantarita, prositabhartrka* and *svadhinabhartika*, are simultaneously and completely present within Srimati Vrsabhanu-nandini. The service of Srimati Vrsabhanusuta to Krishna is incomparable. Only She is capable of giving Krishna complete bliss. Just as Krishna has expansions from Himself, Sri Vrsabhanunandini also has expansions from Herself (*kaya-vyuha*). The eight main *sakhis* of Sri Radha, each dominantly representing one of the eight heroines, are Lalita, Visakha, Citra, Campakalata, Tungavidya, Indulekha, Rangadevi and Sudevi. The eight *sakhis*, each with 16,000 assistants, are engaged in the service of Sri Vrsabhanusuta. Without the association of the pure devotees of the Lord, the deep secrets of this world of service cannot be realized in the least. By not being dependent upon the pure, knowledgeable practitioners of this type of service or by coming under the illusion of immature so-called pure devotees, the *prakrta-sahajiyas* have created a great disturbance due to their lack of knowledge, systematic practice and qualification.

In describing the glories of associating with pure devotees, Srila Prabhupada quotes verses such as:

*sādhavo hṛdayaṁ mahyaṁ sādhūnāṁ hṛdayaṁ tv aham
mad-anyat te na jānanti nāhaṁ tebhyo manāg api*

ārādhanānāṁ sarveṣāṁ viṣṇor ārādhanaṁ param
tasmāt parataraṁ devi tadīyānāṁ samarcanam

In essence, Srila Prabhupada explained as follows: Even though the devotees of Sri Bhagavan are His energy, in the context of service the energy is more powerful than Bhagavan. This is because if that were not so, the devotees would not be able to serve Bhagavan. The completely independent Bhagavan acts as if He is dependent upon the service of the devotees. Srila Prabhupada explained, *ahaṁ bhakta-parādhīno hy asvatantra iva dvija.* Those who serve Bhagavan in the mood of parenthood as His mothers and fathers know the Supreme Lord to be the one that they must protect and nourish. In reality, if the essence of the object of service is unknown, then actual service is not performed. The best servant waits for the instructions of the object of service; he understands the internal mood of the object of service and renders service. Just as Bhagavan is the indwelling soul of the devotees, the devotees are the indwelling soul of Bhagavan (the *antaryami* of the *antaryami,* the soul of the soul). Certainly, as long as one is overcome by the mood of opulence, this elevated platform cannot be taken into one's heart. Bhagavan does not become lovingly pleased by love which is diluted by opulence (*aiśvarya-śithila-preme nāhi mora prīta*).

āpanāke baḍa māne, āmāre sama-hīna
sei bhāve ha-i āmi tāhāra adhīna

"I am subordinate to the mood of my devotees who consider themselves to be supreme and consider Me to be equal to or lower than them."

The deceitful people who, rather than following in the footsteps of the learned practitioners of elevated service, take to mimicry of the learned practitioners are certainly destined for hell.

With great enthusiasm, as if speaking with a hundred mouths, Srila Prabhupada explained the greatness of the Srimati Vrsabhanunandini's supreme service and explained the concepts of the original form (*svayam-rupa*), the direct expansion *(svayam-prakasa)* and the expansion of the direct expansion *(prakasa-vigraha* of *svayam-prakasa amsa-kala,* etc.). Even though the *svayam-prakasa* Sri Baladeva and His non-different form, Sri Nityananda, are like energies, They are intoxicated in serving the *svayam-rupa* in unlimited forms and unlimited ways; They should be surrendered to. Laksmi-devi, Brahma, Shiva, Narada, Suka, Sanatana and others, *svayam-prakasa* Sri Nityananda, Advaita Acharya, who is Mahavishnu's incarnation, Srivasa and other great personalities, Sri Nanda Maharaja in the mood of parenthood, Sridama and other *vraja-sakhas* in the mood of friendship, *vraja-gopis* in the mood of conjugal love, Sri Varshabhanavi Devi, who is the complete manifestation of all mellows, Sri Rukmini and the other queens, *svayam-prakasa* Sri Balarama, Ananta Deva in the form of Sesa, and the various incarnation of Krishna, each one of them mainly takes on the mood of servitude. All of Them have greater joy in serving the *svayam-rupa*.

Thereafter, in describing the main four expansions of Krishna (*chatur-vyuha*), Srila Prabhupada showed the incompleteness of the explanation of the Shankara school, and showed its insignificance through quoting verses from the *Srimad Bhagavatam* such as *jñāne prayāsamudapasya, śreyaḥ-sṛtim, ye'nye'ravindākṣa, tathā na te mādhava,* etc. He showed how through following the process of receiving the mercy of Bhagavan in the descending process (*avaroha* or *srauta-pathavalamabana*), the truths regarding *svayam-rupa, svayam-prakasa, and svayam-prakasa-prakasa* can vibrantly appear in the heart and explained as follows.

Regardless of how intelligent we are in the world, when we go to sketch the form of Bhagavan using the pencil of our material intelligence, it will just manifest as an incompetent figment of our imagination. However, when Bhagavan will bestow His mercy and manifest His form, then there is no question of there being a presence of an incompetent figment of our imagination. That would be His eternal form. Finding out His original form (*svayam-rupa*) is the desire of Sri Chaitanya (*śrī-caitanya-mano-'bhīṣṭa*). *Svayam-rupa* Sri Chaitanyadeva, out of His mercy, manifests in the form of Krishna and is Himself the establisher of His own desire. Then again, *nityānanda pūrṇa kare caitanyera kāma* – "Nityananda fulfils the desire of Sri Chaitanya." Therefore, *svayam-prakasa* Sriman Nityananda Prabhu is the establisher of the desire of Sri Chaitanya. Sri Chaitanya's *prakasa-vigraha* is Sri Rupa Goswamipada. He is the sun-like *acharya* of the Gaudiya Vaishnavas. Life is a success if one is able to become his follower. Sri Rupa Goswamipada, an ocean of that mindset, established the desires of Sri Chaitanya through the four acts of composing devotional literatures, discovering the lost holy places, establishing deities of the Lord and preaching the devotional scriptures. When will we have the fortune of getting a bit of pollen from his lotus-like feet?

Day 3
14 February 1936

In the evening, Srila Prabhupada spent an hour and a half describing the words *preyah* and *sreyah* at Sri Yogapith as follows:

In terms of *preyah* (temporary happiness), we run towards those elements which seem pleasurable, but which are actually not good in the long term. That through which we get true, eternal benefit is known as *sreyah*. That which we like and that which is beneficial based on if something occurs are both dependent on independence. Two streams come from independence, *sreyah* and *preyah*. Wherein *sreyah* and *preyah* have become one, meaning that service to the Lord has become one's object of happiness, is a situation where everything is good for us. When *preyah* is merged into *sreyah*, then our true auspiciousness takes place. If we avert *sreyah* and take up *preyah*, we will be put in an unfavorable circumstance. There is no act apart from doing that which is favorable for Krishna in the situation where *sreyah* and *preyah* have become one. Searching for one's own self-pleasure is filled with *preyah*. There is no tinge of *sreyah* therein. Love for Bhagavan is not subject to incompleteness or deterioration with time. Where there is straightforward service to Bhagavan, therein the bliss that one takes for oneself which is *preyah* actually is *sreyah* for us. By giving up *sreyah* and only running behind *preyah*, we develop envy towards Bhagavan and become demoniac. In order to remove all facilities for Bhagavan, we try to remove the deity form of the Lord and become impersonalists.

In the materially bound condition, there is a difference between *sreyah* an *preyah*. However, in the liberated state, *sreyah* and *preyah* become one. As a result of that, there is no other duty other than service to Bhagavan. Those who are going after *sreyah*, their prayer is:

tat te'nukampāṁ su-samīkṣamāṇo
bhuñjāna evātma-kṛtaṁ vipākam
hṛd-vāg-vapurbhir vidadhan namas te
jīveta yo mukti-pade sa dāya-bhāk

The living entity faces happiness and sadness due to the result of *karma*. Those who have accepted the *sreyah* analysis understand all the results of *karma* to be the mercy of Bhagavan, and by accepting those results, offer obeisance to the lotus feet of Sri Bhagavan through body, mind and words. Rather than praying to become free from the results of *karma*, the living entity prays for causeless service to Bhagavan. In this manner, those who have taken shelter of the path of *sreyah* are qualified to obtain the lotus feet of Bhagavan.

The prayer of those on the path of *sreyah* is clearly shown in this verse of the *Mukunda-mala-stotram*:

nāhaṁ vande tava caraṇayor dvandvam advandva-hetoḥ
kumbhī-pākaṁ gurum api hare nārakaṁ nāpanetum
ramyā rāmā mṛdu-tanu-latā-nandane nābhirantuṁ
bhāve bhāve hṛdaya-bhavane bhāvayeyaṁ bhavantam

The devotees of Bhagavan do not pray to the divine feet of *Sri* Bhagavan for deliverance from the horrible Kumbipaka and Naraka hellish conditions. They also do not pray to enjoy with the beautiful women of the celestial garden, Nandanakanana. They constantly think of the divine feet of Bhagavan in the Vrindavan of their cleansed hearts to experience the love of Bhagavan.

Those who are on the *sreyah* path, are just as devoted to the devotees as they are to Bhagavan. Shambhu, who is the spiritual master, has shown this point in the verse *ārādhanānāṁ sarveṣām.* The spiritual master also offers respect to the disciples. Thus, Shambhu has addressed Parvati as Devi and said, "In comparison to all types of worship, what to speak of worshiping relatives related to one's body, even in comparison to worshiping other gods and goddesses, worship of Vishnu is supreme. Even better than worship to Vishnu is serving the devotees of Vishnu."

Taking shelter of Bhagavan is one thing, and going forward on one's path in the name of service to Bhagavan is another. He who speaks on the path of *sreyah* and sings the glories of Vishnu and the Vaishnava is a true teacher. One who does not do this and teaches anything else is bad association. The scriptures have said *tato duḥsaṅgam-utsṛjya satsu sajjeta buddhimān.* There are many so-called friends who are ready to take us to the liquor shop and the brothel. Such people will stop the talk of Bhagavan and take our minds towards temporary happiness. There is no dearth of such people. Knowing such people to be bad association, one should leave such persons' association completely. Those who constantly engage in the service of Bhagavan and inspire others in the service of Bhagavan are real *sadhus.* One should associate with such people. One should remember:

> *gurur na sa syāt sva-jano na sa syāt*
> *pitā na sa syāj jananī na sā syāt*
> *daivaṁ na tat syān na patiś ca sa syān*
> *na mocayed yaḥ samupeta-mṛtyum*

"Death has to be overcome. It is not overcome on the *preyah* path. Rather, death is invited like the sound of a frog that invites a snake. Death is overcome only on the path of *sreyah.* A *guru* is not a *guru*, a relative is not a relative, a father is not a father, a mother is not a mother, a god is not a god, and a husband is not a husband if he cannot deliver his disciple, relative, son, offspring, worshipper and wife, respectively, from death."

In other words, those who are not on the *sreyah* path of devotion and who are travelers on the path of *preyah* are not qualified to be called *gurus*, relatives and so on. Association of such people who are unqualified and turned away from Bhagavan should be avoided in all ways.

> *sei se parama bandhu sei mātā-pitā*
> *śrī-kṛṣṇa-caraṇe yei prema-bhakti-dātā*
> *sakala janame pitā-mātā sabe pāya*
> *kṛṣṇa-guru nāhi mile bhajaha hiyāya*

Devotees of Bhagavan are never immoral. Those who are averse to the service of Bhagavan are immoral because they do not abide by the main rule, which is to always remember Vishnu and to never forget Him — *smartavyaḥ satataṁ viṣṇur vismartavyo na jātucit*. One should know that the association of all such people is bad association and should give it up. Knowing that so-called morality deals with pleasing one's own senses rather than loving Bhagavan, the devotees of Bhagavan do not associate with such ideologies.

One who says to worship Bhagavan is the spiritual master. is the spiritual master. *Yogis* or *jnanis* looking for *paramatma* or *brahma-jnana* are not on the actual path of *sreyah*. If there is a difference between *paramatma* and *brahma*, then there is no need to go near such a *brahma* or *paramatma*. This is because that line of thought is born from atheism. The association of *brahma-jnani mayavadis* and bad *yogis* (*kuyogis*) is to be avoided. One should associate with *bhakti-yogis*. Devotees are *sadhus*, as they constantly sing the names of Krishna.

harer nāma harer nāma harer namaiva kevalam
kalau nāsty eva, nāsty eva, nāsty eva gatir anyathā

ceto-darpaṇa-mārjanaṁ bhava-mahā-dāvāgni-nirvāpaṇaṁ
śreyaḥ-kairava-candrikā-vitaraṇaṁ vidyā-vadhū-jīvanam
ānandāmbudhi-vardhanaṁ prati-padaṁ pūrṇāmṛtāsvādanaṁ
sarvātma-snapanaṁ paraṁ vijayate śrī-kṛṣṇa-saṅkīrtanam

While preaching, he sings:

kṛṣṇa! kṛṣṇa! kṛṣṇa! kṛṣṇa! kṛṣṇa! kṛṣṇa! kṛṣṇa! he!
kṛṣṇa! kṛṣṇa! kṛṣṇa! kṛṣṇa! kṛṣṇa! kṛṣṇa! kṛṣṇa! he!
kṛṣṇa! kṛṣṇa! kṛṣṇa! kṛṣṇa! kṛṣṇa! kṛṣṇa! rakṣa mām!
kṛṣṇa! kṛṣṇa! kṛṣṇa! kṛṣṇa! kṛṣṇa! kṛṣṇa! pāhi mām!
rāma! raghava! rāma! raghava! rāma! raghava! rakṣa mām!
kṛṣṇa! keśava! kṛṣṇa! keśava! kṛṣṇa! keśava! pāhi mām!

The devotees pray: "O Radharamana! Protect me. Please don't make me return to this mundane existence and destroy myself." Those who have entered the *samsara* would pray, "O Bhagavan! Let me not become too attached to material life. Let my desire for material life be destroyed. Let my focus always be on rendering service to you. Protect me."

Mirate Sil played the kathi and sang: *hare murāre madhukaiṭabhāre gopāla govinda mukunda śaure.*

Various people see the Supreme Truth in various ways according to their qualification. He deceives the *mayavadis* and shows them the form without quality (*nirvisesa*), meaning *mayavadis* are incapable of having *darsana* of *svayam-rupa* because they are offenders at the lotus feet of that *svayam-prakasa-tattva*. When *Svayam-prakasa* Balarama and *svayam-rupa* Sri Krishnachandra, the younger brother of Balarama, went to the wrestling arena of Kamsa, then various people saw them in various ways:

mallānām aśanir nṛnāṁ nara-varaḥ strīṇāṁ smaro mūrtimān
gopānāṁ sva-jano 'satāṁ kṣiti-bhujāṁ śāstā sva-pitroḥ śiśuḥ
mṛtyur bhoja-pater virāḍ aviduṣāṁ tattvaṁ paraṁ yoginām
vṛṣṇīnāṁ para-devateti vidito raṅgaṁ gataḥ sāgrajaḥ

Bhagavan is unparalleled in strength, power, beauty and so on. The living entities cannot even be compared to Him. When Sri Krishna and His elder brother, Balarama, arrived at the wrestling arena of Kamsa, the big wrestlers under whose pride the whole world trembled saw the fierce, hard bodies of Krishna and Balarama. When the normal public saw Sri Krishna, they thought Him to be the best of all men. To the women, Krishna was the living form of cupid. The cowherd men saw Krishna as their very own. To the kings, Krishna seemed as the rightful giver of punishment. To Vasudeva and Devaki, Krishna seemed like their own son. To the worshiper of five gods and to Kamsa, who believed in a quality-less god, Krishna appeared as death personified. To the ignorant people, Krishna appeared as a fathomlessly huge form. To other *yogis*, Krishna appeared as the supreme spiritual truth. To the *vrshnis*, Krishna appeared as the spiritual god.

Day 4
15 February 1936

Srimad Bhagavatam is the essence of all scriptures and is unparalleled. In the very first *mangalacarana* (invocation) verse is present the purport of all the 18,000 verses that follow. The expansion of that verse is the four essential verses of the *Srimad Bhagavatam* (*catuh-sloki*), and the expansion of those four verses is the entire *Srimad Bhagavatam*. *Srimad Bhagavatam* should be heard from and in the shelter of a *sad guru*. The *shruti* scriptures state: *tad-vijñānārtham̐ sa gurum evābhigacchet samit-pāṇiḥ śrotriyam̐ brahma-niṣṭham,* to learn that science, one must go to a *guru* who is learned in scriptural knowledge and is fixed in spiritual realization.

The Thakura Bhaktivinoda Research Institute has been established near Srivas Angana in Sridham Mayapur. It is known as a temple for researching Krishna. Therein, the reason for Mahaprabhu's message being supreme in comparison to all messages will be shown through comparing various philosophies. Topics discussing the speciality of supreme devotion (*uttama-bhakti*), which is free from other desires, work, knowledge and designations, is favorable towards Krishna, and which is characterized by serving Hrshikesa through all the senses, are available there. Srila Prabhupada, in reply to Mr. Banerjee's question on *daiva-varnasrama*, quoted the verse *dvau bhūta-sargau loke 'smin daiva āsura eva ca viṣṇu-bhaktaḥ smṛto daiva āsuras tad-viparyayaḥ.*

In discussing the verse, they discussed Syria, Esyria, Huns and Hamajatis. Discussion on establishing Daiva-Varnasrama-Dharma-Sangha took place as well.

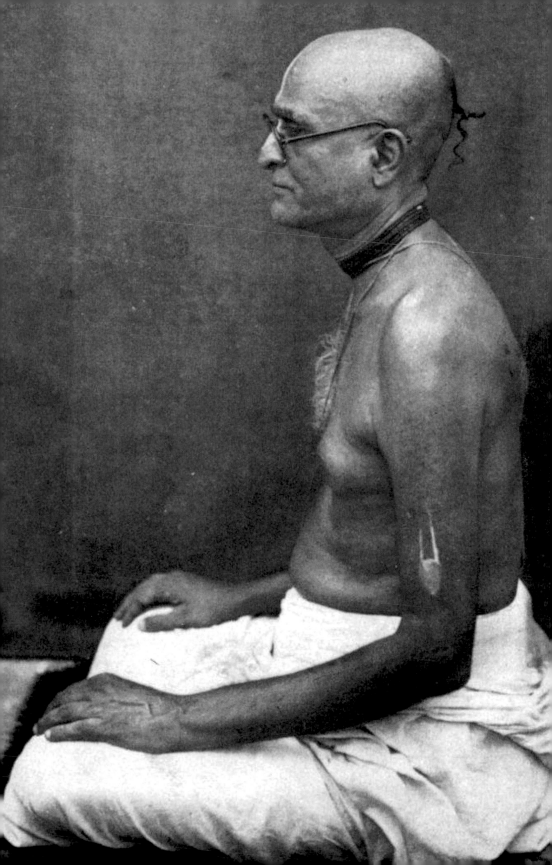

Day 5
16 February 1936

In the glorious assembly, many people have spoken many things. Much time has passed hearing these talks. I do not have much to say. My words have been expressed through their talks. Many have spoken in the English language. Thus, it is necessary for me to speak in the Bengali language. Then again, my Bengali is not so simple. I don't know if it will be understandable to all people. [Note: For this reason, translating the Bengali into English was also a challenge. Please excuse any errors or omissions.]

Firstly, I have to explain why I listened to all of these glorifications of myself all the while. I lack the knowledge of language; despite that, the previous spiritual masters have mercifully made me hear all these glorifications, and my own lack of qualification has been identified therein.

From my side, the purest explanation is that if I had spoken about myself, then I would be responsible for that. However, the glories of my own spiritual masters have been spoken through the mouths of others, and I am not responsible for that. Regarding the behavior I am speaking about, if it were my own behavior, then it would be subject to criticism by others. However, that behavior is not performed by me. It is the work of my spiritual master. Therefore, even if this is seen negatively by others, I am bound to accept it.

We have heard that a tree manifests from a seed. Otherwise, the tree would not be. A seed comes from a tree, and then a tree comes from that seed. If our analysis is that should the tree not produce seeds, then progress will be stopped, and future progeny will not exist, then based on this analysis, I am bound, *ājñā gurūṇāṁ hy avicāraṇīyā* (the order of the *guru* is not to be analyzed);

in following Sri Gurudeva's instruction, I have to sit like an intelligent person and listen to glorifications. If one thinks that listening to glorifications of himself is a good thing, then only his disqualification will be exposed.

In order for the current *harikatha* to continue without cessation, I have to accept this respect and worship. There is a difference between us and those who listen to their own glorifications for the sake of becoming proud.

We should one-pointedly listen to the glories of Sri Guru. I have to accept the way in which my *gurudeva* feels is necessary for me to be. Thus, I am not ready to accept the result of whatever problems come about.

I have heard that we must listen while being more humble than a blade of grass. Sri Guru Pada-padma is he who speaks the glories of Bhagavan. The disciple's prerogative is to listen to the glories which are spoken. Through this *kirtana* and *sravana* from Sri Gurudeva, all these topics blossom in the hearts of the disciples. Even I have become qualified to hear all these talks as a disciple; it is of much importance to learn how to approach Bhagavan and His devotees with humility and how to glorify and respect them.

Today, I found many things to be learned. I learned how to not expect respect for myself and give respect to others. I learned how to put inertia to a stop and how to glorify Sri Bhagavan and His devotees.

It is necessary to glorify the devotees of Bhagavan. The devotees present, deserving worship, have taught us how to glorify Bhagavan and His devotees by presenting glorifications of me as their *gurudeva*. Glorifying the non-devotees and the glorifiers of non-devotees are both problems. My most respectable spiritual masters have taught me humility and are taking care to purify my heart. They have said, "Give respect to the people of the world in all ways just as we have given respect to you, and stay engaged in the service of the devotees. In this way, effulgently serve them."

The opportunity to learn how the object of prayers (*vandya*) is offered prayers (*vandana*) is present. We have heard from the words of our previous spiritual masters:

jagāi mādhāi haite muñi se pāpiṣṭha
purīṣera kīṭa haite muñi se laghiṣṭha

"I am more fallen than a worm in stool and more sinful than Jagai and Madhai."

In this way, when the words through which the spiritual master offers prayers to the object of prayers take effect in the heart, then we know how unqualified we are. It is known from the way they teach about humility and following in the footsteps of the previous teachers that it is impossible to approach Bhagavan and His devotees without these qualities.

If we become proud, then we will be eternally bereft of service.

arcayitvā tu govindaṁ
tadīyān nārcayet tu yaḥ
na sa bhāgavato jñeyaḥ
kevalaṁ dāmbhikaḥ smṛtaḥ

"If there is not devotion towards the devotees to the same degree as there is devotion to Bhagavan, then we have become useless; life has become a waste."

te vai vidanty atitaranti ca deva-māyāṁ
strī-śūdra-hūna-śabarā api pāpa-jīvāḥ
yady adbhuta-krama-parāyaṇa-śīla-śikṣās
tiryag-janā api kim u śruta-dhāraṇā ye

Regardless of how unqualified and inauspicious I am, many devotees have appeared to bestow auspiciousness upon me. Many devotees have appeared to destroy my pride. They are all teaching me how to serve Bhagavan. The day when we are able to totally become free from the evil intelligence of wanting respect from the devotees of Bhagavan and from the greed of wanting the favors that come with the respect from others, we will receive Bhagavan's mercy. We will gain devotion to Bhagavan and become fortunate. Giving an unqualified person qualification will make the person free from his unqualified state. Even though women and *sudras* are seen in a very low position in the eyes of the world due to their work, they become qualified for eternal auspiciousness simply by seeing the devotees and following their teachings and mood of not expecting respect but instead offering respect to all.

arcayitvā tu govindaṁ
tadīyān nārcayet tu yaḥ
na sa bhāgavato jñeyaḥ
kevalaṁ dāmbhikaḥ smṛtaḥ

Taking shelter of devotion, if one become proud and thinks to only worship Bhagavan and not the devotees, then various problems will arise due to having committed this offense at the feet of the devotees.

Why do we forget that the human form of life is not to collect inauspiciousness but rather to gain the supreme auspiciousness? Why do I forget that I am the most fallen compared to all? The idea of wanting to enjoy the senses, being tempted by *maya*, and the idea of wanting to become great are totally insignificant and unnecessary. If it is necessary to gain the inclination to become great in the world, to gain true welfare, then Vaishnava ideals should be accepted. Qualified people have enough strength from service and are strong. I have not gained so much strength that I shall become engaged in finding the faults of the Vaishnavas and their behavior. I will not reject the way service is done and establish my own opinion.

There is nothing left to be said about how such practices will totally destroy one's human life. I am holding your two feet and speaking with utmost humility – please do not mimic behavior; follow in the footsteps of the Vaishnavas. We should not keep the association of anyone other than devotees. Association with those who are not devotees can increase each of our desires to satisfy the senses.

Many years, one by one, have passed for me. I have understood that I do not have any other path except for the lotus feet of the Vaishnavas. Each of my activities is subject to attack. Thus, to those who see me as a lowly person, this is my prayer to them: If they think that they shall follow in the footsteps of the Vaishnavas, then they will no longer have such negative ideas. They will compassionately give strength to the foolish, unlearned, weak people; they will infuse energy within the people.

One who serves Hari considers himself to be most fallen in comparison to all. When one thinks himself to be the most fallen, then one can become the best Vaishnava. He can speak the supreme topics about devotion to Hari.

sarvottama āpanake hīna kari māne

If one thinks he is supreme, one should test one's own disqualification. Without testing one's own self, why is there so much inclination to find the faults of others? Is this the nature of the Vaishnava? On the other hand, in the vision of the Vaishnava, even he who is not elevated, is elevated.

yady adbhuta-krama-parāyaṇa-śīla-śikṣās
tiryag-janā api kim u śruta-dhāraṇā ye
vaisnavera kriya mudrā vijneha nā bujhaya

Devotees are intensely devoted to Bhagavan. We do not come under illusion by apparent or external realities. Through external analysis, people fall down, due to illusion, thinking an oyster to be a pearl, thinking a rope to be a snake, and seeing inauspiciousness in auspiciousness. When people are overcome by illusion, then in the view of the outside world, all of the senses become eager to fulfill the lack of the external world. How to be delivered from this condition of *maya* is to be analyzed. If I think, "The devotees of Bhagavan have taken up a slave mentality, and I will take up the Lord's mentality to fulfill this lacking," then nothing good will come of that. With that type of mindset, being controlled by the senses, one has to go forward on the path towards hell.

If I disrespect the devotees of Bhagavan in order to gain my own supremacy, then I will be thrown into a three-dimensional jail and be forced to run towards vastness from narrowness. "I will become good. My disease will be cured. Let there be auspiciousness." These types of ideas are good. However, ideas such as "I will become great. I will stop everyone else in the world, and let my envious attitude be successful" – such a mindset is not laudable at all. It is not correct to take away the worshipful status of devotees while trying to establish one's own greatness. The *srauta* path has corrupted due to the wrong explanation of the *aham brahmāsmi* aphorism. I have heard the actual meaning of this aphorism from my spiritual master, which is:

tṛṇād api sunīcena taror api sahiṣṇunā
amāninā mānadena kīrtanīyaḥ sadā hariḥ

How many great people are present here today? How humble they are! We gain so much from hearing their talks. We receive auspiciousness. From the *Talavakara Upanishad*, we have gotten the understanding that those who want to become the master of the master of the devotees are extremely arrogant. The *Srimad Bhagavat* says:

jānanta eva jānantu kim bahūktyā na me prabho

Of all paths present in the world, not even one will lead to Bhagavan. Trying to become the Lord of the devotees of Bhagavan is the path to hell. Going on that path leads to inauspiciousness.

Following in the footsteps of the devotees leads to auspiciousness. All arrangements to go on that path are favorable.

ādadānas tṛṇam dantair
idam yāce punaḥ punaḥ
śrīmad rūpa-padāmbhoja-
dhūliḥ syām janma-janmani

Even if it be life after life, let us be the dust at the lotus feet of the devotees of Bhagavan following in the footsteps of the process given by Sri Rupa! The root of this understanding is to realize one's own lack of qualification. If the understanding of "I have no qualification" comes from one's own self or through someone else, then we will be able to look towards the beauty of the lotus feet of the devotees of Bhagavan. The general public is concerned with how sense gratification can be fulfilled. If we think that to be the path of *dharma*, then we will be unable to become true followers of *dharma*.

Everyone worships the divine feet of Bhagavan; however, the ideology of "Bhagavan, give me so and so facility" is nothing but business. "What will I get in exchange for what?" Such an ideology is not held by the devotees of Bhagavan. If one tries to follow such an ideology, he will be unable to understand service to Krishna. Bhagavan is supremely auspicious. Rather than praying to Him for supreme auspiciousness, if we pray to Him for the fulfillment of selfish desires, then that is not the sign of intelligence. One should follow the ideology which explains the way in which Krishna is to be served.

kāmādīnāṁ kati na katidhā pālitā durnideśās
teṣāṁ jātā mayi na karuṇā na trapā nopaśāntiḥ
utsṛjyaitān atha yadu-pate sāmprataṁ labdha-buddhis
tvām āyātaḥ śaraṇam abhayaṁ mām niyuṅkṣvātma-dāsye

O, Bhagavan! Engage me in Your service. I am no longer able to serve dogs, horses, iron, gold, humans or gods. There is only one way to be liberated from the utter self-destruction that I am faced with today, having served them – that is, through service to You (*dasya*). However, it is almost impossible to obtain service to You without serving those who have surrendered their very selves in Your service. Service to the devotees gives the most auspiciousness in all respects.

We are unable to see Bhagavan here. The devotees who serve Bhagavan bestow their mercy on us and give us the ability to see Bhagavan. Their activities are to be followed, and they are our one and only way towards auspiciousness. Due to having very little knowledge, many people, out of their own insignificant experience, try to equate the mentality of the devotees of Bhagavan to that of a slave mentality. Let those who speak from a state of mental aberration speak whatever they please. However, our understanding will be:

parivadatu jano yathā tathā vā
nanu mukharo na vayaṁ vicārayāmaḥ
hari-rasa-madirā-madāti-mattā
bhuvi viluṭhāma naṭāma nirviśāmaḥ

We will roll in the foot dust of the devotees. We will not make anybody our disciple; we have not and we shall not either. This is because, if it happens, then we will run in the wrong direction due to being tempted by the tastes of non-devotees. All of you are my spiritual masters. Have mercy on this fallen soul, thinking him to be your disciple."

PART TWO

DIVINE AGENTS

His Divine Grace Srila Bhaktisiddhanta Saraswati Goswami Thakura Prabhupada's contribution to spreading the loving message of Sri Krishna Chaitanya Mahaprabu was invaluable, and, in the form of his disciples, he gave the world so many shining rays (special exalted personalities). As described earlier, these rays were promised and sent to Srila Prabupada by Sri Krishna Chaitanya Mahaprabhu Himself from the Lord's eternal abode to fulfill His predication: "My name shall spread in every town and village around the world."

Srila Prabhupada and his rays were extraordinary beings, and their entire lives serve as living examples and epitomes of Vaishnava qualities and etiquette. His rays, being the "manpower" sent by the Lord, continued to spread the loving message of Sri Krishna Chaitanya Mahaprabhu after Srila Prabhupada's departure.

They established many Gaudiya Vaishnava institutions with different names and branches, founded by different *acharyas*. For example,

- Sri Gopinath Gaudiya Math founded by His Divine Grace Srila Bhakti Pramode Puri Goswami Maharaja
- Sri Chaitanya Gaudiya Math founded by His Divine Grace Srila Bhakti Dayita Madhava Goswami Maharaja
- Sri Chaitanya Saraswat Math founded by His Divine Grace Srila Bhakti Rakshak Sridhar Dev Goswami Maharaja
- International Society for Krishna Consciousness (ISKCON) founded by His Divine Grace Srila Bhaktivedanta Swami Goswami Maharaja
- Sri Krishna Chaitanya Mission founded by His Divine Grace Srila Bhakti Vaibhava Puri Goswami Maharaja
- Sri Krishna Chaitanya Math founded by His Divine Grace Srila Bhakti Kamal Madhusudan Goswami Maharaja

- Sri Gaudiya Vedanta Samiti founded by
  His Divine Grace Srila Bhakti Prajnan Keshava
  Goswami Maharaja

They also continued to manage Sri Gaudiya Math (also known as Sri Chaitanya Math), established by Srila Prabhupada, which over the years had the following Presidents:

- His Divine Grace
  Srila Bhakti Saranga Goswami Maharaja,
- His Divine Grace
  Srila Bhakti Kevala Audulomi Goswami Maharaja,
- His Divine Grace
  Srila Bhakti Srirupa Bhagavat Goswami Maharaja,
- His Divine Grace
  Srila Bhakti Hridaya Bon Goswami Maharaja,
- His Divine Grace
  Srila Bhakti Vivek Bharati Goswami Maharaja,
- His Divine Grace Srila Bhakti Srirupa Siddhanti
  Goswami Maharaja,
- His Divine Grace
  Srila Bhakti Mayukh Bhagavat Goswami Maharaja,
- His Divine Grace
  Srila Bhakti Vilas Tirtha Goswami Maharaja, etc.

All the disciples of Srila Prabhupada were pure devotees of Sri Sri Radha Krishna. In this chapter, a brief summary is provided on the life, nature and achievements of some of Srila Prabhupada's rays, where such information was available.

CHAPTER SIX

SRILA BHAKTYALOKA PARAMAHAMSA GOSWAMI MAHARAJA

On Thursday, 4 May 1893 (Bengali calendar: 22 Vaishakh 1300), a transcendental baby was born to landowner Sri Kalikumar Singha-Chaudhury and Srimati Chandravali Devi in the village of Bhavanipur, Ramaganj, Noyakhali, Bangladesh. They named the baby Mahendra Kumar Singha-Chaudhury. Mahendra Kumar had transcendental qualities and was a jewel of society. After completing his schooling at the village's primary school, he went to Bagerhat College in Khulna, Bangladesh for higher studies.

Since his childhood, he was always eager to serve Lord Hari. During his studies, Srila Prabhupada came to Bangladesh, and Mahendra Kumar was able to meet with him. After he met Srila Prabhupada, his eagerness to serve Lord Hari increased and he decided to leave his studies and go to Calcutta and then Mayapur to meet with Srila Prabhupada again. He devoted himself to serve Sri Sri Guru Gauranga Gandharvika Giridhari Jiu, the first deities established by Srila Prabhupada. In a short period of time, Mahendra Kumar's service skills attracted all of the devotees surrounding Srila Prabhupada. He received initiation and the name Sri Mahananda Das Brahmachari. He had firm faith in chanting *harinama* and also possessed Vaishnava qualities such as incredible humility, a soft nature and extreme tolerance.

After initiation, on Gaura Purnima day, during the *Visva Vaishnava Raja Sabha* function, Srila Prabhupada gave him the title 'Bhaktyaloka' (devotional beacon / guiding light) in front of everyone. During his *brahmachari* life, Mahananda Brahmachari looked after the Bhagavat printing press at Krishnanagar, which printed the *Nadia Prakash* and various periodicals of Srila Prabhupada. He was also part of the management team at Sri Chaitanya Math (Adi Math). After Srila Prabhupada's physical departure, Mahananda Brahmachari went to his godbrother, Vinode Bihari Prabhu (later known as Srila Bhakti Prajnan Keshava Goswami Maharaja, the founder of Sri Gaudiya Vedanta Samiti) and assisted him in every aspect for a long time. Thereafter, he went to another godbrother, Srila Bhakti Bhudev Shrauti Goswami Maharaja, and served at Sri Gaura Sarasvat Math at Jhargram, West Bengal.

On Monday, 17 May 1954 (3 Jaistha 1361) on Sri Jagannathadev's Snana Yatra (the annual bathing ceremony of Lord Jagannath), Sri Mahananda Das Brahmachari was inspired to take *sannyasa* initiation from his godbrother Srila Bhakti Rakshak Sridhar Dev Goswami Maharaja, founder-acharya of Sri Chaitanya Saraswat Math, Kolerganj, Navadwip, Nadia. After *sannyasa*, his name became Srila Bhaktyaloka Paramahamsa Goswami Maharaja. In 1957, Srila Bhakti Swarupa Parvat Goswami Maharaja, founder of Sri Varshabhanavi-dayita Gaudiya Math, Udala, Mayurbhanj, Odisha, physically departed from this world. Thereafter, Srila Paramahamsa Goswami Maharaja became the *acharya* (initiating guru) of this *math*. He gave spiritual instructions and initiation to everyone without discrimination in terms of caste and creed.

Then Srila Paramahamsa Goswami Maharaja went to Calcutta at Gauranga Premartha Pracarini Sabha, which is situated at 106 Hazra Road, Calcutta. He spent a long time at this center. Srila Bhakti Rakshak Sridhar Goswami Maharaja, Srila Bhakti Pramode Puri Goswami Maharaja and other godbrothers used to meet with Srila Bhaktyaloka Paramahamsa Goswami Maharaja at this center. During his stay at Calcutta, Srila Bhakti Rakshak Sridhar Dev Goswami Maharaja gave Srila Paramahamsa Goswami Maharaja a land in Mayapur to establish a temple. As per the request of his godbrother, before his physical departure Srila Paramahamsa Goswami Maharaja established a temple at Ishodyan, Mayapur in the name of Sri Paramahamsa Gaudiya Math. In Navadwip, Gauranga is Krishna and Gadadhar is Radharani. He established Sri Sri Gaura Gadadhar deities in his temple in Mayapur. The Gaura Gadadhar deities are the *bhajan-vigraha* (the deities representing internal development and service to Sri Sri Radha Krishna).

Srila Bhaktyaloka Paramahamsa Goswami Maharaja physically left the world from Sri Mayapur Dham to enter into the eternal pastimes of Sri Gaura Gadadhar at 4:20 after the *mangala arati* of the deities on Tuesday, 8 November 1983 (22 Kartik 1390). His *samadhi* is located inside the Paramahamsa Gaudiya Math temple, where the Gaura Gadadhar deities are present. After his departure, one of his renounced female disciples, Pratima Devi Dasi, looked after the temples. His disciple Sri Nitai Das Prabhu took *sannyasa* from Srila Bhakti Pramode Puri Goswami Maharaja and received the name Srila Bhakti Sadhak Nishkinchan Goswami Maharaja. Later, Srila Nishkinchan Goswami Maharaja became the *acharya* (initiating *guru*) of Sri Paramahamsa Gaudiya Math.

Srila Bhakti Bhudev Shrauti Goswami Maharaja

One of the personalities sent to Srila Prabhupada by Lord Chaitanya was Ram Gopal, who would later be known as Srila Bhakti Bhudev Shrauti Goswami Maharaja. Ram Gopal appeared on Monday, 2 February 1894 (21 Magh, fifth day of the waxing moon cycle), as the eldest son of Sri Ramsundar Chattopadhyay and Saraswati Devi in Chhatna, Bankura, West Bengal.

To fulfill the mission of Srila Prabhupada, Ram Gopal, aged 35, came to Sri Chaitanya Math in Mayapur on Friday, 20 April 1928 (7th Baishak 1335). Shortly afterwards, Srila Prabhupada gave him *harinama* and *diksha* (first and second initiation). His service attitude for Chaitanya Mahaprabhu's mission was most attractive. Therefore, two years later, on Tuesday, 23 September 1930 (7 Ashwin 1337), Srila Prabhupada bestowed *sannyasa* initiation upon him, with the name Bhakti Bhudev Shrauti Goswami Maharaja. He was the sixth *sannyasi* disciple of Srila Prabhupada.

Seeing his skills in every area of spiritual practice, Srila Prabhupada appointed him as the assistant editor of the Bengali daily publication the *Dainik Nadia Prakash*, and the publisher of the *Bhagavat Patrika*, a magazine printed in the Hindi and Oriya languages. Srila Shrauti Maharaja was proficient in Hindi, Oriya, Bengali, Sanskrit and English.

After *sannyasa*, Srila Prabhupada sent him to preach across India and spread the loving message of Lord Chaitanya. In 1932, Srila Prabhupada instructed him to establish a temple in Varanasi, Allahabad (Prayagraj) and Gaya. By nature, Srila Shrauti Maharaja was always engaged in one service after another all over India. Therefore, many devotees would say that he was an incarnation of Narada. Srila Shrauti Maharaja established temples in Jhargram, Tata Nagar, Bolpur, and Birbhum.

Srila Shrauti Maharaja departed from the material world on Monday, 10 January 1983 on the auspicious day of Dvadashi (29th Poush). His exemplary service attitude will always be an inspiration for us devotees to continue our service.

Srila Prabhupada would say that Srila Bhakti Bhudev Shrauti Goswami Maharaja is a valuable asset of Lord Chaitanya's mission.

SRILA BHAKTI DAYITA MADHAVA GOSWAMI MAHARAJA

Srila Bhakti Dayita Madhava Goswami Maharaja is one of Sri Chaitanya's spiritual descendants. He appeared in a superior *brahmana* family on 18 November 1904 at 8.00 in the village of Kanchanpara, district Faridpur (Subdivision – Madaripur), Bangladesh. His parents, Sri Nishikanta Devsharma Bandyopadhyay and Srimati Shaivalini Devi, named their new son Heramba Kumar Bandyopadhyay. He was nicknamed Ganesh by his family.

Sri Heramba appeared in this world on the most auspicious day of Utthana Ekadasi, a day that is deemed auspicious by the entire Gaudiya Vaishnava community. It was on that same lunar-cycle day that Srila Gaura Kishore Das Babaji Maharaja, a prominent descendant of Lord Chaitanya, departed from this world. In order to fill the gap, Lord Chaitanya sent Sri Heramba here to this world.

Since childhood, Sri Heramba was extraordinarily expert in academics. He also felt greatly inclined to acquire the association of a pure devotee of the Lord and left home at a young age to travel to the Himalayas. While returning from the Himalayas, He stayed in Haridwar for some days. During that time, an economically rich but childless couple wanted to adopt Heramba as their son and offered to bequeath their entire property to him. This lucrative offer did not deter Heramba's mind from his spiritual goal. Eventually, in 1925, Sri Heramba came to Mayapur with his friends and met with his *gurudeva*, Jagad-guru Srila Prabhupada. Two years later, on 4 September 1927, Sri Heramba received initiation at No-1, Ultadingi Junction Road at Calcutta on the auspicious day of Sri Radhashtami. He became known as Sripad Hayagriva Das Brahmachari.

Seeing Sripad Hayagriva Prabhu's service attitude, Srila Prabhupada used to say that he had amazing volcanic energy. Once, Srila Prabhupada asked Hayagriva Prabhu, "What makes you extremely happy?" Sripada Hayagriva Prabhu answered, "Srila Prabhupada, when you give me a service which I have not yet been able to complete but again you order me to do an additional service, that makes me extremely happy."

When Srila Prabhupada physically departed from this world, all his disciples felt a turmoil in their spiritual practices due to their pangs of separation from him. Due to Sripad Hayagriva Prabhu's attractive and exemplary preaching skills, many people wanted to take shelter of him. Eventually, Sripad Kunjabihari Vidyabhushan, who was later known as Srila Bhakti Vilas Tirtha Goswami Maharaja, as well as all the other godbrothers, requested Sripad Hayagriva Prabhu to give shelter to all aspiring devotees.

In order to fulfill the desire of Lord Chaitanya, Sripad Hayagriva Prabhu took *sannyasa* initiation from his very dear senior godbrother Srila Bhakti Gaurav Vaikhanas Goswami Maharaja at Tota Gopinath temple located in Puri, Odisha on the auspicious day of Gaura Purnima in 1944. He received the name Srila Bhakti Dayita Madhava Maharaja.

In 1953, Srila Madhava Goswami Maharaja, in a non-sectarian and non-judgmental mood, established a spiritual society named Sri Chaitanya Gaudiya Math, solely to provide a base for all devotees to practice spirituality. His affection for all his godbrothers was spontaneous. He often used to say, "Even if it is required for me to beg from door to door for the service of my godbrothers, I will do so." He welcomed all his godbrothers to stay in his society without hesitation, and some of them did until they established their own societies.

Srila Madhava Goswami Maharaja's broad vision was to make people understand the real goal of spiritual practice. Once, a businessman came to Mayapur and approached Srila Madhava Goswami Maharaja to open a brick manufacturing factory on his agricultural field. The businessman said, "Here in Mayapur, many temple constructions are going on which will require bricks. You can sell them bricks and get enough money to manage your institutional activities. You can use the leftover bricks from the factory for constructing your temple." After hearing this proposal, Srila Madhava Goswami Maharaja told him, "Seth ji Mahashay, your proposal is very good. You are proposing to make a poor materially detached *fakir* (an ascetic subsisting solely on alms) into a rich (*amir*) materially attached person. However, the goal of my society is to change the rich materially attached, *amir*, into the poor materially detached, *fakir*. Your proposal is materially attractive, but for us it is not acceptable."

Gradually, Srila Madhava Goswami Maharaja's attractive preaching skills inspired many people to follow Lord Chaitanya's mission. He established many centers around prominent cities in India. Many spiritually advanced devotees, such as Srila Bhakti Ballabh Tirtha Goswami Maharaja, Sri Bhakti Vigyan Bharati Goswami Maharaja, Sri Bhakti Sundar Narsingha Maharaja, Sri Bhakti Suhrit Damodar Goswami Maharaja, Sri Bhakti Lalit Giri Goswami Maharaja, Sri Bhakti Prasad Puri Goswami Maharaja and many others joined and helped him expand Lord Chaitanya's mission.

Once, Gurupada Das, an economically poor householder devotee from Bengal, who was a disciple of Srila Bhakti Hridaya Bon Goswami Maharaja, came to Sri Chaitanya Gaudiya Math in Calcutta. It was midday when he arrived, but everyone had already completed their lunch *prasadam*. Gurupada Das told a devotee who was residing at the temple that he would like to meet with Srila Madhava Goswami Maharaja. Upon hearing that Srila Bon Goswami Maharaja's disciple Gurupada had arrived, Srila Madhava Goswami Maharaja personally came downstairs to meet him. Seeing that such a great *acharya* had come downstairs to meet him, Gurupada was completely astounded and immediately offered his obeisance. In a sweet voice, Srila Madhava Goswami Maharaja asked, "What service can I do for you?" When the devotee heard those words, he felt shy hearing such words coming from the mouth of such an exalted devotee. Then he spoke, "Actually, my spiritual master, Srila Bhakti Hridaya Bon Goswami Maharaja, is permanently staying in Vrindavan, but I don't have any money to go to Vrindavan to meet with my Gurudeva and take *diksha* initiation. I have only taken *harinama* initiation from him, and I desire to take *diksha* initiation from you, if you will mercifully allow me to."

After these words of the devotee, Srila Madhava Goswami Maharaja loudly laughed and embraced Gurupada. He said, "You are my spiritual nephew. I can do that only if my godbrother, Srila Bon Goswami Maharaja, orders me. Then, I can give you *diksha* on his behalf." Thereafter, Srila Madhava Goswami Maharaja arranged for the devotee's *prasadam*. Gurupada went home and eventually was able to arrange money to go to Vrindavan and take initiation from his Gurudeva, Srila Bon Goswami Maharaja. This shows the loving relationship, generosity and simplicity of Srila Madhava Goswami Maharaja.

Before his physical departure from this world, Srila Madhava Goswami Maharaja appointed Srila Bhakti Ballabh Tirtha Goswami Maharaja on 30 December 1978 as his successor in order to continue with Lord

Chaitanya's mission. Maharaja left this world physically on 27 February 1979 in the Calcutta temple. According to his wishes, his disciples took his physical body from Calcutta to Mayapur and placed him in a *samadhi* there on the premises of Sri Chaitanya Gaudiya Math.

Srila Madhava Goswami Maharaja's entire life was exemplary of the main goal of Lord Chaitanya's mission: the real meaning of sincerity, generosity, magnanimity, purity and simplicity.

CHAPTER NINE

SRILA BHAKTI GAURAV VAIKHANAS GOSWAMI MAHARAJA

To establish the ritualistic procedures, one significant spiritual soul appeared in Odisha in a landlord (*zamindar*) *brahmana* family in Badagada village, Ganjam District on 23 October 1877 (Bengali calendar: 8 Kartik 1284 Krishna Pratipada, 1st day of the waning-moon cycle). As per astrological calculations based on the time of his birth, his father, Jadumani Rath and his mother, Lalita Devi, named their newborn baby Ujjwaleshwar Rath. Since his childhood, Ujjwaleshwar was always grave and silent, symptoms of an intellectual and spiritually realized soul. He was not very much absorbed in material studies but always came first in his class. Ujjwaleshwar was well versed in economics, logic, philosophy and political science. His family members were royal priests (*raja-purohits*) for the king of Odisha. Once, the king of Odisha heard about Ujjwaleshwar's charismatic excellence and called him to debate with an assembly of royal scholars (*raja-pandit-mandali*). Ujjwaleshwar defeated all the royal scholars and was awarded the title, 'Patta-joshi'. Thereafter the king appointed Ujjwaleshwar as his royal priest (*raja-guru*).

Once, a miracle took place with Ujjwaleshwar as follows. A royal priest named Lingaraj Mishra from another kingdom, named Dharakot, wanted to teach *tantra* (a kind of black magic) to Patta-joshi Ujjwaleshwar. It was the new-moon day, and they went to the cremation ground. According to Lingaraj Mishra's direction, Patta-joshi Ujjwaleshwar sat on a dead body and chanted some *mantra*. Suddenly, the dead body became alive and moved. Lingaraj Mishra (who was a *tantric-guru*) ran away in fear. However, Patta-joshi Ujjwaleshwar continued sitting fearlessly and chanting the *mantra*. As he chanted the *mantra*, the dead body became calm, and a ghostly spirit began speaking from the body. The ghost (*pretatma*) said, "Why are you here in the cremation ground and doing such *sadhana* (practice)?" Patta-joshi Ujjwaleshwar replied, "I want transcendental knowledge *(para-vidya)*." Then, the ghost said, "You will soon meet an exalted spiritual personality, and he will fulfill all of your desires." After speaking, that ghost left the dead body.

Another miraculous incident took place with Patta-joshi Ujjwaleshwar, the king and his associates. Once, they were all traveling in the forest. By evening, they were all tired. In order to take rest, they all went to a hermitage near a village. People practicing black magic *(tantra)* lived in that hermitage. The *tantrics* hosted everybody. The king and his associates took rest. A few minutes later, the head *tantric* of the hermitage called everyone for dinner. Patta-joshi Ujjwaleshwar had some doubt about how dinner was arranged so quickly. Patta-joshi Ujjwaleshwar took some *kusha* grass, chanted some *mantras*, made rings out of the grass and had everyone wear the grass rings. He then said, "Touch whatever food the head of the hermitage will offer you with this grass ring before eating." Upon following his instructions, they found that all the food miraculously turned into stool when touched by the grass rings. After that incident, Patta-joshi Ujjwaleshwar took some yellow mustard seeds, chanted some *mantra*, and destroyed all the power of the black magic *tantric* people. After this incident, the king glorified Patta-joshi Ujjwaleshwar's power and gave him an award.

On another occasion, whilst travelling deep into the forest, the king and his associates were tired and hungry. They all took shelter under the shade of a big banyan tree. After sunset Patta-joshi Ujjwaleshwar chanted some *mantras* and created a hut and a tribal person. That tribal person collected many fruits and roots and fed everyone. Everybody took rest and passed the night there. In the early morning, the king told Patta-joshi Ujjwaleshwar, "Last night, we had such nice fruits and roots and rested nicely. I would like to offer an award to that tribal person who helped us." As he looked in the direction of the hut, the king noticed that the hut and tribal person were no longer there. All he saw was the deep forest as it was when they had arrived there, and he found himself sitting under that same tree. The king was astonished and asked Patta-joshi Ujjwaleshwar, "What is this? How did this happen?" Patta-joshi Ujjwaleshwar just laughed. The king understood that these miraculous activities all happened by the power of *raja-guru* Ujjwaleshwar's *mantra*.

In 1921, Patta-joshi Ujjwaleshwar was jailed, as he was part of M. K. Gandhi's non-cooperation revolution for the independence of India from British rule. Hearing the words of Patta-joshi Ujjwaleshwar and noting his behavior and effulgent form, within a short space of time the governor of the jail was motivated from within his heart to release Patta-joshi Ujjwaleshwar.

Once, Patta-joshi Ujjwaleshwar was traveling by train to Vrindavan. It was a cloudy day, and the sun was not visible. Patta-joshi Ujjwaleshwar had taken a vow never to eat anything before seeing the sun. He began to chant verses glorifying the sun. Within some time, the clouds passed and the sun shone brightly in the sky. As Patta-joshi Ujjwaleshwar thought about what to eat, the train stopped at a railway station. An old man carrying a basket of fresh fruit came and gave him the whole basket and then disappeared. Patta-joshi Ujjwaleshwar was thinking who this old man could be and how he could pay him for the fruit. After some time, Patta-joshi Ujjwaleshwar heard a voice from the sky, which spoke, "I am the sun god, Suryadeva. You were hungry so I came and gave you fruits. Just eat the fruits." Immediately, Patta-joshi Ujjwaleshwar offered his obeisance to Suryadeva and begged for forgiveness since he had personally come and offered his service to Patta-joshi Ujjwaleshwar. Then, he thought that he should first offer the fruit to the Lord. Patta-joshi Ujjwaleshwar decided to wait until reaching Vrindavan to offer the fruit to Govinda, Gopinath and Madanmohan, and thereafter, he honored the *prasadam*.

Patta-joshi Ujjwaleshwar once went to a village for some work. It was already evening, and he felt tired as he was returning from his work. He was searching for a place to take rest, and the villagers showed him a deserted, haunted house where he could rest. Secretly, the villagers just wanted to test his powers. Whilst he was taking rest, a ghost who was previously a *brahmana* (*brahma-daitya*) appeared in his vision. Patta-joshi Ujjwaleshwar asked him, "Who are you?" The *brahma-daitya* said, "I am a *brahma-daitya* ghost (spirit soul with no body)." Patta-joshi Ujjwaleshwar asked, "Why are you coming here? What do you want?" The *brahma-daitya* ghost replied, "You are my food. I would like to eat you." Patta-joshi Ujjwaleshwar said, "Why do you want to eat me?" The ghost replied, "Whoever comes to this house is food for me." Patta-joshi Ujjwaleshwar asked, "What benefit will you get by eating me? You will still remain a ghost. Rather you please think about how you can become delivered from this sinful condition." Then, the ghost said, "Who can deliver me?" Patta-joshi Ujjwaleshwar said, "I will deliver you from this sinful condition. Thereafter, please worship Lord Hari. In this way, you will attain auspiciousness." The *brahma-daitya* ghost agreed. Patta-joshi Ujjwaleshwar took some water from his water pot (*kamandalu*), chanted some *mantras* and offered the pious benefit of one of his own Ekadashi fasts to the ghost and sprinkled the water on him. Immediately, the ghost was delivered from its ghostly existence, circumambulated Patta-joshi Ujjwaleshwar and traveled northwards in the sky, having attained deliverance. Patta-joshi Ujjwaleshwar then went to sleep.

The next morning the villagers were surprised to find him sleeping peacefully in that haunted house. They could not understand how he was so peaceful, as they were aware of the presence of the ghost in that house. As the villagers spoke amongst each other, Patta-joshi Ujjwaleshwar awoke. They thought that he may have turned into a ghost and began shouting, "Ghost! Ghost!" Then, Patta-joshi Ujjwaleshwar told them, "Don't be afraid. I am the same Patta-joshi." He explained the events that had taken place the night before. The villagers were ashamed that they had planned to test his powers. They realized how powerful Patta-joshi Ujjwaleshwar was, as he had not only survived but had also delivered the ghost from the haunted house.

Patta-joshi's ultimate desire was to gain transcendental realization of the Supreme Lord. In 1924, the Lord fulfilled his desire when Srila Prabhupada made his auspicious arrival along with his associates in Ganjam, Odisha. After hearing the discourses of Srila Prabhupada and his associates, Patta-joshi Ujjwaleshwar developed faith towards the Gaudiya Math and Sri Krishna Chaitanya Mahaprabhu.

In 1932, Srila Prabhupada traveled from Calcutta to Mayapur by boat along with his associates. Patta-joshi Ujjwaleshwar was part of the group of devotees traveling with Srila Prabhupada. Patta-joshi Ujjwaleshwar had the habit of chewing betel leaves. Whilst travelling, he spat in the Ganga River. At that time, Srila Prabhupada explained the glories of the Ganga. After hearing all of the glories of the Ganga, Patta-joshi Ujjwaleshwar felt guilty and ashamed of his action. He asked for forgiveness from mother Ganga and took his entire container of betel leaves and placed it at Srila Prabhupada's divine lotus feet. When they reached Sri Chaitanya Math in Mayapur, they visited all the holy places of Lord Chaitanya's pastimes. He approached Srila Prabhupada for *harinama* and *diksha* initiations. He mercifully agreed and gave him both initiations simultaneously. From that time on, he stayed with Srila Prabhupada in Sri Chaitanya Math.

One day at Sri Chaitanya Math, Ujjwaleshwar Prabhu asked Srila Prabhupada, "To whom should I go to learn *Srimad Bhagavatam* in your absence?" Srila Prabhupada replied in a grave voice, "You should learn the message of the *Srimad Bhagavatam* from Ramdas Prabhu." Ujjwaleshwar Prabhu was searching for Ramdas Prabhu and found him weeding the agriculture field while chanting the Hare Krishna *maha-mantra*. Seeing Ramdas Prabhu's constant chanting, Ujjwaleshwar Prabhu realized the actual mood of Vaishnavism.

On 1 March 1934, Gaura Purnima day, Srila Prabhupada gave Ujjwaleshwar Prabhu *sannyasa* initiation and the new name Srila Bhakti Gaurav Vaikhanas Maharaja. According to the desire of Srila Prabhupada, a *sankirtan* hall named Sri Brahma Madhva Gaudiya Shravan Sadana was constructed in Bhanjanagar, Odisha under the supervision of Srila Vaikhanas Goswami Maharaja. Once Srila Prabhupada wanted to arrange a one-month-long program during Kartik month where many devotees would come together and listen to discourses on Lord Hari at Purushottam Math located at Chatak Parvat, Sri Jagannath Puri Dham. Srila Vaikhanas Goswami Maharaja was responsible for successfully making all the arrangements. Upon reaching Purushottam Math, Srila Prabhupada was astonished to see the first-class arrangements that had been made and bestowed his blessings upon Srila Vaikhanas Goswami Maharaja.

On another occasion in the Manjusha Village in Srikakulam, Andhra Pradesh, an assembly was arranged to discuss Brahmanism versus Vaishnavism. The royal priest of the kingdom was trying to establish that *brahmanas* were superior to Vaishnavas. After everybody spoke and established that point, Srila Vaikhanas Goswami Maharaja remembered the lotus feet of Srila Prabhupada and eloquently explained, with scriptural evidence, that a *brahmana* who has realized the Supreme Absolute Truth (*Brahman*) and engages in the worship of that Supreme Lord is known as a Vaishnava. After hearing Srila Vaikhanas Goswami Maharaja's logical explanation about the superiority of Vaishnavas over *brahmanas*, everybody began glorifying him, chanting, "Jay! Jay!" In this way, Srila Vaikhanas Goswami Maharaja served Srila Prabhupada's mission, pleasing him greatly.

After Srila Prabhupada's disappearance, Srila Vaikhanas Goswami Maharaja served as the principal priest in the *samadhi* ceremony. Srila Vaikhanas Goswami Maharaja established many of the ritual procedures for deity worship in the Gaudiya Math. After Srila Prabhupada's disappearance, Srila Vaikhanas Goswami Maharaja went to Brahmapur, Ganjam District, Odisha for solitary spiritual practice (*nirjana-bhajana*). He lived in a dilapidated, tiny room beside a Sri Sri Radha Krishna temple. He begged and collected alms, which he would cook and eat. He was once a great royal priest and was now happily begging for maintenance whilst upholding his *sannyasa* vow.

In 1950, many reputed persons became Srila Vaikhanas Goswami Maharaja's disciples, and with their assistance, he established a temple at Prem Nagar in Brahmapur named Sarasvata Ashram. In 1959, Srila Vaikhanas Goswami Maharaja left that temple and established one more temple in Gounjanagar, Odisha with the help of a devotee named Krishna Das Prabhu. Gradually, this temple expanded with the help of Srila Bhakti Vaibhava Puri Goswami Maharaja, Srila Bhakti Dayita Madhava Goswami Maharaja,

Anandalilamayavigraha Prabhu, and others. Many of Srila Vaikhanas Goswami Maharaja's godbrothers took *sannyasa* initiation from him, including Hayagriva Prabhu at Tota Gopinath temple (who became known as Srila Bhakti Dayita Madhava Goswami Maharaja), Pranavananda Prabhu at Champahatti Gaura Gadadhar temple (who became known as Srila Bhakti Pramode Puri Goswami Maharaja) and so on. Many of his godbrothers had loving affection for him.

Once, Srila Vaikhanas Goswami Maharaja was at Gounjanagar Ashram, Odisha. He was not physically well and expressed the desire to go to Vrindavan. At that time, one of his godbrothers, Anandalilamayavigraha Prabhu, took Srila Vaikhanas Goswami Maharaja out of his *ashram* to a canal in that village and told him, "This is the Yamuna River"; he showed a nearby forest in the village and said, "This is Vrindavan." In that way, he showed Srila Vaikhanas Goswami Maharaja Vrindavan Dham. Srila Vaikhanas Goswami Maharaja said, "Now, I can leave my body blissfully." Two days after this incident, on 22 January 1966 (Bengali Calendar 8 Magh 1372, Shukla Pratipada, first day of the waxing-moon cycle) at midday, Srila Vaikhanas Goswami Maharaja left this world at the age of 95 and entered into the eternal pastimes of Sri Sri Radha Govinda. He was placed into *samadhi* in the *ashram* campus.

Srila Bhakti Gaurav Vaikhanas Goswami Maharaja is an exemplary Vaishnava personality who shows us how to surrender from a royal priestly position to a mendicant beggar taking up the vow of *sannyasa*. Srila Vaikhanas Goswami Maharaja's personality teaches us how to be free from all material designations and gradually become established in our eternal service until we are delivered from this miserable world and attain the ultimate goal of divine love for Sri Sri Radha Govinda.

CHAPTER TEN

SRILA BHAKTI HRIDAYA BON GOSWAMI MAHARAJA

On 23 March 1901 (Bengali calendar: 11 Chaitra 1307), a very special child was born to father Rajanikanta Mukhopadhyay and mother Dakkhinakali Devi in Baharpur village, Dhaka district, Bangladesh. The baby was named Narendranath Mukhopadhyay; Nasu was his nickname. His father was a master in Astrology, a rigid *brahmana* and the village leader. Everyone in the village had sound faith and respect for this family. A few Vaishnavas used to chant the Lord's names while playing the *mridanga* and *karatals* around the village. Rajanikanta taught his son that they were traditional Vaishnavas and devotees of Krishna.

Since his childhood, Narendranath had spontaneous attraction towards the Vaishnavas, and he would only take *prasadam*. He used to follow all the rules and regulations of rigid *brahmanas*. When neighbors and relatives asked the little boy, "Narendranath, what is your goal in life?" Narendranath replied, "I want to be a real *sadhu*."

When Narendranath was five years old, his father enrolled him in a traditional Vedic school (*pathasala*) where Narendranath learned to recite all the traditional Vedic literatures. Then, his father, Rajanikanta, brought him to an English medium school for higher studies in Telirbag village. His teachers were extremely happy to see Narendranath's talent in his studies. Eventually, he completed his IA degree in deductive and inductive logic from Patna University with distinctions and also completed an honors degree in the English language.

After receiving his academic degree, Narendranath was not feeling any satisfaction and felt that he needed some spiritual potency to become blissful. As a result, he was aloof from society. Once, his father, Rajanikanta, became ill. As per the doctor's advice, Narendranath came with his father to Dhaka, Bangladesh. Serendipitously, Narendranath found the Madhva Gaudiya Math and

saw a picture of Srila Prabhupada. As soon as he saw the picture, he felt some internal connection and asked the local devotees, "Who is this?" The devotees replied, "This is Prabhupada, our *gurudeva*. He lives in Calcutta."

In 1925, in order to get some medicine for his father's treatment, Narendranath went to Calcutta with one of his relatives. He sent the medicines back to Dhaka and remained in Calcutta to meet Srila Prabhupada. When he arrived at Srila Prabhupada's Calcutta center at No. 1 Ultadingi Junction Road, he first met with Sundarananda Vidyavinode Prabhu.

After three days, Srila Prabhupada came to the Calcutta center from his preaching tour. Upon seeing Srila Prabhupada, Narendranath immediately realized and thought, "He is my eternal shelter, my most worshipful *gurudeva*." Narendranath heard spiritual discourses in Srila Prabhupada's room. Within an hour of the discourse, Narendranath wrote an entire article based on all of Srila Prabhupada's points that were explained in that discourse. The article was entitled "Who is our real relative?" Srila Prabhupada was astonished and immediately told Sundarananda that this article must be published in the upcoming edition of the weekly *Gaudiya Patrika*.

After a few days, Narendranath's brother, Vishweshwar Mukhopadhyay, came to the Ultadingi center to take Narendranath back to Dhaka. However, as soon as Vishweshwar saw Narendranath's *shikha*, shaved head, *dhoti* and complete Vaishnava attire, he became angry. Vishweshwar tried in vain to take Narendranath back to Dhaka.

In 1925, when Narendranath was 24 years old, Srila Prabhupada gave him *harinama* and *diksha* initiations, simultaneously, and the new name, Nandasunu Brahmachari. After a few months, seeing Nandasunu

Brahmachari's preaching skills, Srila Prabhupada gave him the renounced order (*sannyasa* initiation) on Friday, 4 September 1925 (Bengali calendar: 19 Bhadra 1332) and the new name Tridandi Swami Bhakti Hridaya Bon Maharaja. In order to spread the loving mission of Lord Chaitanya, Srila Bon Goswami Maharaja went out and preached all over India.

In 1933, Srila Bon Goswami Maharaja was one of the first disciples whom Srila Prabhupada sent to the West by ship, namely to London, England, Hamburg, Germany, and Vienna, Austria to spread the loving message of Lord Chaitanya. Srila Bon Goswami Maharaja spoke to many prestigious government audiences and university gatherings.

In one of his discourses, he very attractively spoke about how pure love cannot be established with any living entity on this planet but rather, can only be established with the embodiment of pure love who is the Supreme Lord Sri Krishna. Srila Bon Goswami Maharaja explained how the only way to attain God is through constantly chanting the Hare Krishna *maha-mantra* while being non-duplicitous, simple, pure, free of offenses and free of material desires.

Srila Bon Goswami Maharaja even preached to Adolf Hitler. In 1941, in Calcutta, the government officials took Srila Bon Goswami Maharaja to court and questioned him about why he met with Hitler. In reply, Srila Bon Goswami Maharaja said that he had explained the same message to Hitler which he had spread in different universities and prominent government offices.

After this incident, Srila Bon Goswami Maharaja went to the four holy places, namely Kedarnath, Badrinath, Gangotri and Yamunotri and performed intense spiritual practices there before returning to Vrindavan. In 1948, he established the Institute of Oriental Studies in Vrindavan in order to bestow accredited degrees and education to the local population. In 1952, upon seeing Srila Bon Goswami Maharaja's skill in *shastra* and his purity, the *acharyas* of the four *sampradayas* appointed him, during the Allahabad Kumbha Mela, as the *mahanta* of the four *sampradayas*. In 1960, Srila Bon Goswami Maharaja represented India at the UNESCO International Congress of the History of Religion.

After the departure of Srila Bhakti Vilas Tirtha Goswami Maharaja (Kunjabihari Vidyabhushan), Srila Bon Goswami Maharaja was elected as the next *acharya* of Sri Chaitanya Math, Mayapur and its branches. He served as *acharya* for some time. After his health deteriorated, he retired to Vrindavan to his temple called Bhajan Ashram situated near Madanmohan Gehra.

A few days before his physical departure after *mangala arati* in his Vrindavan temple, he called all his disciples and said, "None of you should come in my room or touch my bed. A chariot will come from Goloka Vrindavan and take me to the spiritual world. None of you should be sad and cry. I am always with you. When I depart with the *sakhis* to Goloka, you should see me off with smiling faces." Srila Bon Goswami Maharaja is Latika Manjari in the spiritual world.

At 21:00 on Thursday, 7 July 1982 (Bengali Calendar: 22 Ashadh 1389), Srila Bon Goswami Maharaja departed from this world in his Vrindavan temple. His *samadhi* is located there. Presently, his dear disciple Srila Gopananda Bon Goswami Maharaja is the *acharya*, continuing the mission. Srila Bhakti Hridaya Bon Goswami Maharaja's entire life is an example of renunciation according to time, place and circumstance. If anyone follows in his footsteps, that person will definitely become free from all material attachments and be delivered from this miserable material world.

CHAPTER ELEVEN

SRILA BHAKTI JIVAN JANARDAN GOSWAMI MAHARAJA

1918 is a very significant year for all Gaudiya Vaishnavas as, in that year, Srila Prabhupada Bhaktisiddhanta Saraswati Goswami Thakura completed chanting one billion holy names and also established the Gaudiya Math. In the same year, Srila Janardan Goswami Maharaja appeared in Ganjam district, Odisha, India. Due to Srila Maharaja's humility, we are not getting any information about his family details. His disciples barely managed to get the following information.

Srila Prabhupada's mission was started in order to spread the loving message of Lord Chaitanya. Therefore, Srila Janardan Maharaja, at an early age (an internet article states that he left home at the age of seven) left home and eventually, came to the shelter of his *gurudeva*, Srila Prabhupada.

After joining the Chaitanya Math in Mayapur, he was fully dedicated to serving all Vaishnavas. He used to attend discourses given by various *sadhus* (disciples of Srila Prabhupada), *mangala arati, sandhya arati* and so on with sound faith. Seeing such faith in him, the devotees attested this to Srila Prabhupada about Maharaja's devotional attitude. After hearing the devotional glories of the small boy from different Vaishnavas, Srila Prabhupada gave him *harinama* and *mantra diksha* on an auspicious day and named him Sri Ananta Rama Das Brahmachari.

After this initiation, Srila Prabhupada kept Sri Ananta Rama Das Brahmachari as his own dear personal servant. He was engaged by Srila Prabhupada to study devotional books under his senior godbrothers. He would listen to Srila Prabhupada's *harikatha* very attentively. Gaining inspiration from *harikatha*, Ananta Rama Prabhu began to collect alms (*bhiksha*) for the service of *guru* and Vaishnavas. Whenever preachers would come to the temple, Ananta Rama Prabhu used to serve them to the best of his ability. Seeing such a service mood, all the devotees living in the temple liked Ananta Rama Prabhu and bestowed their blessings on him. Most of the time, Srila Prabhupada engaged Sri Ananta Rama Brahmachari at the Gaudiya Math branch in Cuttack, sometimes at Chatak Parvat, Jagannath Puri Dham and sometimes at Bag Bazar Gaudiya Math, Calcutta.

Sri Ananta Rama Das Brahmachari assisted his godbrothers in their preaching. Although he engaged most of the time in serving Vaishnavas and serving in different temples, he also attentively studied *Srimad Bhagavatam, Chaitanya-charitamrita, Chaitanya Bhagavat, Srimad Bhagavad Gita* and the different *Puranas*, etc. He used to recite various *shlokas* from his heart. In this way, he became a great speaker who would always speak with *shastric* evidence.

After Srila Prabhupada's physical departure, Sri Ananta Rama Das Brahmachari used to stay at Chaitanya Math, Mayapur, but due to certain circumstances, he was drawn to associate with like-minded senior godbrothers. So, he left Chaitanya Math and came to Sri Shyamananda Gaudiya Math located in Shiv Bazar, Medinipur. This center was a home rented, for preaching, by a group of Srila Prabhupada's disciples (Bhakti Dayita Madhava Goswami Maharaja, Radharaman Das Brahmachari, who later became Bhakti Kumud Santa Goswami Maharaja, Bhakti Vichar Jajabar Goswami Maharaja and Ananta Rama Das Brahmachari). During his stay at Shyamananda Gaudiya Math, Radharaman Das Brahmachari and Ananta Rama Das Brahmachari became bosom friends and studied different devotional books together. They would also go to the various ancient libraries of

Medinipur and study the different scriptures present there.

Eventually, Ananta Rama Das Brahmachari was told by different godbrothers to take *sannyasa*. In order to follow his godbrothers' instruction, he chose his senior godbrother who used to be the *raja-pandit* of Odisha, Srila Bhakti Gaurav Vaikhanas Goswami Maharaja, to be his *sannyasa guru*. After *sannyasa* initiation, Srila Bhakti Gaurav Vaikhanas Maharaja gave him the name Tridandi Swami Srila Bhakti Jivan Janardan Goswami Maharaja.

As time passed, the godbrothers of Shyamananda Gaudiya Math decided that the *math* should be registered in the name of Bhakti Vichar Jajabar Goswami Maharaja and that the rest of the godbrothers would leave to go out and spread Lord Chaitanya's message of divine love, sharing amicable relations with each other. Thereafter, Srila Bhakti Jivan Janardan Goswami Maharaja established a temple in Khargapur, Subhaspalli, Medinipur, West Bengal.

Srila Janardan Maharaja's sweet and logical discourses quoting different *Puranas* attracted most of the local people from all walks of life who, subsequently, took shelter of Srila Janardana Maharaja. Srila Janardan Maharaja used to serve cows with his own hands at his temple's *goshala*, including cleaning cow dung, offering food to the cows, etc. Srila Janardan Maharaja would blissfully host any holy persons like his godbrothers who came with their disciples and look after them in a loving manner.

He used to, mentally, serve Srimati Radha Thakurani under the shelter of Rupa (Rupa Manjari) and Raghunath(Rati Manjari), Srimati Lalita Sakhi and their associates. Srila Janardan Maharaja would often say to his devotees, "If you really want to establish love for Radha Krishna's services, then you must always remain drowned in the ocean of nectar of the holy names given by Lord

Chaitanya. In mind, you must always serve Srimati Radharani's eternal maidservants, namely Lalita, Visakha, Rupa Manjari, and Ananga Manjari without hypocrisy, with full humility and not desiring respect for yourself." This is the supreme goal of Mahaprabhu's mission. During the time of chanting Hare Krishna *maha-mantra*, Srila Janardan Maharaja used to cry out, "Ha Radhe! Ha Radhe! Ha Visakhe! Ha Lalite! Ha Gaura! Ha Nitai! Ha Prabhupada!" with eyes full of tears. Seeing Maharaja's chanting in this mood of separation, many devotees felt very inspired. Sometimes, they saw him rolling on the ground, calling out in this way.

Srila Janardan Maharaja established two temples: Sri Gauravani Vinodashram and Sri Bhaktisiddhanta

Saraswati Gaudiya Math. The temples had the deities Sri Sri Gaura Radha-Nayanavinoda Bihari Jiu and Sri Sri Gaura Radha Kunjabihari Jiu, respectively. Both temples were established in Khargapur, Medinipur area. In order to offer Radha Krishna's favorite flowers like the jasmine, tuberose, *madhavi, malati,* etc., Srila Narottama Das Thakura wrote in one song, *ganthiya malatira mala diba donhara gale,* which means, "I will make garlands with *malati* flowers to offer to the Divine Couple, Sri Sri Radha-Krishna. Srila Janardan Maharaja's attitude was like this; he used to make the garlands and offer them to Sri Sri Radha Krishna.

Maharaja's loving nature with all of his godbrothers and spiritual nephews made them feel comfortable in associating with him. His godbrothers Bhakti Vaibhava Puri Goswami Maharaja, Bhakti Prajnan Keshava Goswami Maharaja and Bhakti Kumud Santa Goswami Maharaja were his bosom friends. Just prior to his physical departure, Sril Bhakti Jivan Janardan Maharaja appointed Bhakti Kamal Govinda Maharaja, a disciple of Bhakti Vaibhava Puri Goswami Maharaja, as his successor. Due to Bhakti Jivan Janardan Goswami Maharaja's loving attitude, Srila Bhakti Vaibhava Puri Goswami Maharaja's disciple took *sannyasa* from Srila Jivan Janardan Goswami Maharaja in the presence of Srila Bhakti Vaibhava Puri Goswami Maharaja. That disciple's name became Bhakti Vichar Vishnu Goswami Maharaja, and he is presently one of the *acharyas* of Sri Krishna Chaitanya Mission.

Srila Bhakti Jivan Janardan Goswami Maharaja gave us the following important instructions:

1. The one and only way to achieve the Supreme Lord is to cultivate one-pointed, unalloyed devotion for Him. One must have the same type of devotion for

the spiritual master, who is the condensed form of mercy of the Supreme Lord.

2. I have many instructing spiritual masters (*shiksha-guru*) but only one initiating spiritual master (*diksha-guru*), who is one without a second. Everybody can give instructions and teachings; however, only one person can accept me as his own and offer me to the lotus feet of the Supreme Lord.

3. One on the path of devotional practice (sadhana-bhakti) eternally sees the Lord present in all Vaishnavas and lovingly deals with them, offering appropriate respect, reception and service. Such behavior is the life of the devotees who are practicing devotion (*sadhana-bhakta*).

4. A rupanuga is one who practices devotion following in the footsteps of Srila Rupa Goswami and Srila Raghunath Das Goswami; a rupanuga is totally overwhelmed in the mood shown by Sri Rupa and Raghunath in their forms on earth and in the spiritual world. Amongst all the Vaishnavas on earth, a genuine *rupanuga* Vaishnava is extremely rare and supreme.

5. How can those who cannot unitedly serve here, in this world, following in the footsteps of Sri Guru-Vaishnavas, serve in the footsteps of the devotees in the spiritual world? Without following in the footsteps of the devotee, service becomes mundane work. Lack of tolerance and lack of following in the footsteps of the devotees is equivalent to suicide.

6. A life favorable for devotion consists of straightforwardness and simplicity. The sign of Vaishnavism is to not give trouble to any living entities while carrying out one's daily work. Before

instructing others, one must accept and follow the instructions in one's own life.

7. One can gain spiritual qualifications solely through one-pointedly surrendering unto Sri Hari, Guru and the Vaishnavas. One-pointed surrender is the sign of a healthy devotional life. There is no time for independence in the practice of surrender.

8. If practicing devotees do not remain careful about offending Sri Guru, Vaishnavas, the deity, the Holy Name and the holy places, then, even if they perform service and chant the holy names for a long time, it will be impossible for their consciousness to turn away from the desire to enjoy material sense objects. Rather, unwanted material motives and tendencies (*anarthas*), ignorance and various desires that are unfavorable for devotion will gain strength in the heart.

9. Being established in one's relationship with Krishna, being constantly engaged in loving service, and chanting the names of Krishna constantly without deception are the main duty and constitutional function of a servant of Krishna. If this occurs, then one's *chitta* (mind, intelligence, consciousness and heart) will be purified, and it will be possible to attain pure loving devotion (*prema-bhakti*). The Holy Name is the bud of divine love.

10. The extent to which one's absorption in material sense objects decreases is the extent to which that practitioner of devotion gains devotion. As long as one does not develop a true feeling of compassion towards all living entities, one will continue to have a lack of taste in chanting the holy names. Having compassion upon the living entities, understanding

their relationship with the Supreme Lord, is the ornament of the Vaishnava.

11. Genuine chanting of the holy names should be done in the way that was taught by the most merciful Sri Sacinandana Gaurasundara. Sri Vrishabhanu-nandini Radharani is the main blissful potency (*mula hladini*). Without Her mercy, it is impossible to serve Sri Krishna.

12. Sri Gaurasundara is the incarnation of the Supreme Lord, Sri Vrajendranandana, in the form of the spiritual master who teaches by example (*acarya-avatara*). The beauty of Lord Gaurasundara's form, His behavior and preaching, and His unparalleled magnanimity are but a wonder of the extremely merciful sweetness of Sri Vrishabhanu-nandini, who cannot even be reached by the Shruti, Smrti, Puranas, Brahma and the Devas.

13. Srimati Radharani is my master. The dust of Her lotus feet is just like a wish-fulfilling cow (*kama-dhenu*). A particle of transcendental dust of Her lotus feet controls the all-attractive young cupid-like king of all mellows, Sri Shyamsundar. My constitutional function is to be Her servant. The servants of Srimati Radharani are my shelter. Srimati Radharani is most merciful and loves Her servants very much. Sri Radharamana is an unlimited ocean of nectarine mellows; He increases the love of Srimati Radharani. He is the love of my life.

14. Gaining devotion for the Supreme Lord, Sri Krishna, is very rare. Even more rare than that is to gain devotion for becoming the servant of Srimati Radharani, who is the form of supreme ecstatic bliss. Under the shelter of the spiritual master in his

form as a sakhi, one gains the desire for becoming the servant of Srimati Radharani.

15. Becoming the servant (*dasi*) of Srimati Radharani is even more glorious than becoming one of Srimati Radharani's friends (*sakhis*).

The abovementioned valuable spiritual instructions are coming from the holy lips of Srila Bhakti Jivan Janardan Goswami Maharaja.

At the age of 76, on Monday 5 December 1994 (18 Agrahayana 1401) at 6:15 A.M. during the third day of the waxing moon, Srila Bhakti Jivan Janardan Goswami Maharaja departed from this world from Sri Gauravani Vinodashram Gaudiya Math, Subhaspalli, surrounded by his disciples and other devotees who were loudly chanting the Hare Krishna *maha-mantra*. Maharaja left his body while chanting, "Ha Radhe! Ha Krishna! Ha Prabhupada!" Srila Janardan Maharaja's exemplary service attitude for Sri Guru, Vaishnava and Bhagavan is giving us inspiration to practice humility, tolerance, not expecting respect for ourselves, offering respect to all others, and to serve with our own hands as much as possible instead of just engaging others. He inspired us to chant the Hare Krishna *maha-mantra* while remembering the inner meaning and mood of the pastimes of the transcendental abode.

CHAPTER TWELVE

SRILA BHAKTI KAMAL MADHUSUDAN GOSWAMI MAHARAJA

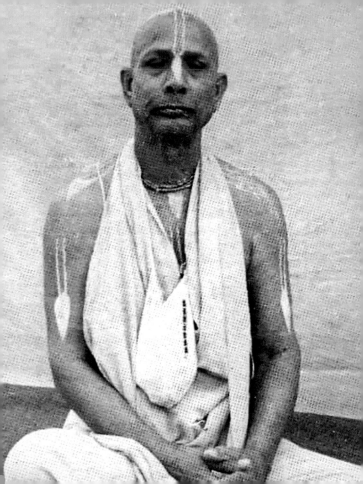

The Supreme Lord Krishna in the form of Sri Krishna Chaitanya Mahaprabhu draws many blessed souls from different parts of India and abroad in order to spread His loving message. One of those blessed souls appeared in a *brahmana* family in Bajitpur village, Faridpur District, Bangladesh on Thursday 19th December 1901 (Bengali calendar 4 Poush 1308). His parents, Parvatinath Sanyal and Swarnamayi Devi, named him Nripendranath. Since childhood, he was grave by nature, renounced, had sound faith in the Lord and was anointed with all spiritual qualities. He studied in his village school.

In 1921, Nripendranath moved to Calcutta for higher studies at Calcutta City College. In 1925, he graduated and was hired as the assistant editor of the English newspaper *Amrita Bazar Patrika*. During his lunch break, Nripendranath used to go to the Gaudiya Math situated at No. 1 Ultadingi Junction Road and listen to discourses on the *Srimad Bhagavatam* given by Pranavananda Brahmachari, who was later known as Srila Bhakti Pramode Puri Goswami. Eventually, Nripendranath developed sound faith in the teachings of the Gaudiya Math and met with Srila Prabhupada Bhakti Siddhanta Saraswati Goswami Thakura. After meeting Srila Prabhupada, Nripendranath decided to take shelter of this effulgent personality.

In 1929, he took initiation from Srila Prabhupada and got the name Sri Narottamananda Das Brahmachari. Srila Prabhupada sent Narottamananda Brahmachari along with his *sannyasa* disciples to preach. In 1932, Srila Prabhupada was on a preaching tour in Mumbai. At the time, Srila Prabhupada sent 12 cantos of *Srimad Bhagavatam* from Mumbai to Narottamananda Brahmachari and instructed him to spread the message of the *Bhagavatam* for the rest of his life. From that time onward, Narottamananda gradually developed expertise on the *Srimad Bhagavatam*.

On Gaura Purnima in 1935, Narottamananda received an award from Srila Prabhupada and the title 'Bhakti Kamal,' meaning lotus of devotion.

When Srila Prabhupada physically passed away, Narottamananda experienced great distress and returned to Bag Bazar Gaudiya Math, the place where Srila Prabhupada had left his body. Thereafter, following the instruction of his senior godbrothers, Narottamananda went to Raya Ramananda Gaudiya Math located in Andhra Pradesh. Due to his fruitful preaching abilities, Narottamananda's authorities sent him to Madras Gaudiya Math to spread the message of the *Srimad Bhagavatam* from there. After some time, due to a lack of like-minded devotee association, Narottamananda left Madras Gaudiya Math and moved to Balaji Venkateshwara temple and stayed there for some time before travelling on pilgrimage. In order to help his senior godbrother Srila Bhakti Prajnan Keshava Goswami Maharaja, Narottamananda spent some time as a preacher in Srila Keshava Goswami Maharaja's mission.

In 1952, Narottamananda Das Brahmachari took *sannyasa* initiation from his senior godbrother Srila Bhakti Rakshak Sridhar Goswami Maharaja and received the name Srila Bhakti Kamal Madhusudan Goswami Maharaja. Srila Madhusudan Goswami Maharaja preached under the guidance of Srila Sridhar Goswami Maharaja and became the chief editor of the *Sri Gaudiya Darshan* monthly magazine published from Srila Sridhar Goswami Maharaja's Sri Chaitanya Saraswat Math.

In 1962, Srila Madhusudan Goswami Maharaja established a new temple named Sri Krishna Chaitanya Math in Mithapukur, Burdwan, West Bengal. In 1974, Srila Madhusudan Goswami Maharaja established another temple, in Mayapur, which is presently located next to Sri Gopinath Gaudiya Math. Srila Madhusudan

Goswami Maharaja's charismatic discourses on *Srimad Bhagavatam* drew many spiritually inclined people to take shelter of him. By nature, he was very meticulous in his spiritual practice, and he trained his disciples accordingly.

According to the tradition of the Gaudiya Math, all renounced male devotees must shave their heads and beards on *purnima* (full-moon day); devotees are not allowed to shave only their beards and not their heads. One *brahmachari* refused to shave fully. Srila Madhusudan Goswami Maharaja immediately asked him to leave the temple and informed all other centers to not accommodate this *brahmachari* in any of the centers. Srila Madhusudan Goswami Maharaja was very strict and particular in spiritual practices and followed Srila Prabhupada's instructions and example precisely.

Srila Madhusudan Goswami Maharaja was very simple by nature. He was appreciated by many of his godbrothers, including Srila Bhakti Vichar Jajabar Goswami Maharaja, Srila Akinchan Krishnadas Babaji Maharaja, Srila Bhakti Dayita Madhava Goswami Maharaja, Srila Bhakti Pramode Puri Goswami Maharaja and so on. Before his physical departure, Srila Madhusudan Goswami Maharaja was totally absorbed in chanting the Hare Krishna *maha-mantra*.

At 15:35 on 20 July 1991, during the Ulto Rath Yatra festival of Sri Baladeva, Subhadra, Jagannath and Sudarshan, when They return from Gundicha Mandir to the Sri Mandir, Srila Madhusudan Goswami Maharaja entered into the spiritual abode from his Mayapur Sri Krishna Chaitanya Math. His *samadhi* ceremony was performed thereafter on his Mayapur temple premises. Srila Madhusudan Goswami Maharaja's entire spiritual practice demonstrates to us how follow the teachings of the *parampara* with our best ability in an uncompromising manner.

CHAPTER THIRTEEN

SRILA BHAKTI KEVALA AUDOLUMI GOSWAMI MAHARAJA

In order to prove that spiritual practice may need a lot of adjustment within our lives, Srila Bhakti Kevala Audolumi Goswami Maharaja, a spiritual descendent of Lord Chaitanya's lineage, appeared on 9 December 1895 (8th day of the waning-moon cycle) in the village of Vanaripara, Barishal district, Bangladesh. His parents were Sri Sarat Chandra Guha and Srimati Bhuvanmohini Devi. His family named him Pramodebihari. Since childhood, Pramodebihari's intellectual ability was attractive in every aspect, academically and spiritually. In academics, he always surpassed everyone in all classes. In 1919, Pramodebihari graduated from Calcutta University.

In 1913, at the age of 18 years old, he met with Sri Bimala Prasad (Srila Prabhupada) at a *Bhagavat* discourse program in Kalighat, Calcutta. After three or four days of hearing Srila Prabhupada's discourses, Pramodebihari got inspired to be connected to the Vaishnava lineage, and Srila Prabhupada happily gave him first and second initiation. He received the name Sri Patitapavan Das Brahmachari.

According to Srila Prabhupada's instructions, Sri Patitapavan Prabhu went to receive the blessings of Srila Bhaktivinoda Thakura personally. Srila Bhaktivinoda Thakura instructed him to read *Srimad Bhagavatam*, the most authenticated scripture for devotional practices.

Due to the loving affection of his mother, Sripad Patitapavan Prabhu felt reluctant to join Srila Prabhupada's mission fully. When his mother, Bhuvanmohini Devi, physically passed away, Sripad Patitapavan Prabhu decided to follow a renounced life. In a short period of time, Srila Prabhupada gave him the devotional title 'Vidyarnava', which means ocean of knowledge. On 17 November 1934, Srila Prabhupada gave him *sannyasa* initiation, and he got the name Sri Bhakti Keval Audolumi Goswami Maharaja. After

sannyasa initiation, Srila Prabhupada appointed him as the principal of Sri Thakura Bhaktivinoda Institute, Mayapur, and simultaneously, engaged him in preaching to foreign visitors who came to Mayapur.

After Srila Prabhupada's departure, following the instructions of Srila Prabhupada and Srila Bhaktivinoda Thakura Srila Audolumi Goswami Maharaja started to preach extensively all over India under the shelter of Srila Puri Das Thakura, who was previously known as Sripad Ananta Vasudeva Prabhu. After Srila Bhakti Pradip Tirtha Goswami Maharaja's physical departure, on the order of Srila Puri Das Thakura Srila Audolumi Goswami Maharaja abandoned his saffron robes of *sannyasa* and accepted the white attire of a *babaji*, which is known as the fifth stage of the Vaishnava renounced order. After an unavoidable incident in February 1954, Srila Bhakti Kevala Audolumi Goswami Maharaja was appointed by Srila Puri Das Thakura as *acharya* of the entire Gaudiya Mission. Also, in this time, his eternal identity of Sri Vinodini Manjari was spontaneously revealed in his heart.

In 1958, Srila Audolumi Goswami Maharaja established a temple in the name of Sri Bhaktisiddhanta Saraswati Gaudiya Math just next to Srila Bhaktivinoda Thakura's Bhajan Kutir in Godrumadwip, the island which represents the performance of *sankirtan*. For almost 28 years, Srila Bhakti Kevala Audolumi Goswami Maharaja ecstatically conducted devotional programs in all the branches of the Gaudiya Mission. On 6 January 1982, Srila Audolumi Goswami Maharaja left the mortal world to join the eternal pastimes of Sri Radha Krishna. His transcendental body was given samadhi inside the temple campus of Sri Bhaktisiddhanta Saraswati Gaudiya Math, Godrumadwip.

SRILA BHAKTI KUMUD SANTA GOSWAMI MAHARAJA

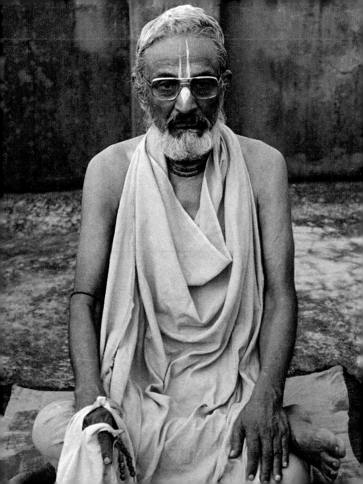

Amongst the many significant rays of Srila Prabhupada, one of them was a little boy named Radharaman Prabhu. On 15 April 1914, before sunrise, Radharaman Prabhu appeared to his devotee parents, Sripad Vaikunthanath and Srimati Ratnamayee Devi, at the village of Narma, district Medinipore, West Bengal. His parents were both householder disciples of Srila Prabhupada.

Upon invitation to Narma Sanskrit Society's annual function, on behalf of Sri Gaudiya Math a few exalted individuals attended, including Pranavananda Das Brahmachari (later known as Bhakti Pramode Puri Goswami Maharaja), Bhakti Hriday Bon Goswami Maharaja and other brahmacharis. Radharaman's parents happily hosted them. Radharaman Prabhu was 11 years old at the time. The two preachers noticed the spiritual qualities of Radharaman. Upon their request, his father happily sent Radharaman to serve his *gurudeva*, Srila Prabhupada. Srila Prabhupada allowed him to resume his academic study at Calcutta and later on to study Sanskrit under the guidance of Gaur Das Pandit in Mayapur.

In 1930, when Radharaman was 16 years old, Srila Prabhupada gave him *harinama* (first initiation) and engaged him to manage a huge spiritual exhibition from 3 February to 17 March. In 1931, Srila Prabhupada gave him saffron attire. In 1933, in order to spread the loving message of Lord Chaitanya, Srila Prabhupada sent Srila Bhakti Hridaya Bon Goswami Maharaja along with Radharaman Prabhu to Bangladesh. Upon returning from the Bangladesh preaching tour, Sripad Radharaman Brahmachari Prabhu received *diksha* (second initiation) from Srila Prabhupada at Bag Bazar Gaudiya Math, Calcutta.

TEN UIT
TINGS FROM
SE AUS
LEURS SOUVENIRS D' ~ AMSTERDAM ~ Damrak
Steiger 1,2,3
Tel:245406

For a few years thereafter, Sripad Radharaman Prabhu was responsible for the management of Sri Prapanna Ashram in Howrah Maju. He was also engaged by Srila Prabhupada to preach in various places, including Pakistan and Burma. Observing his charismatic service attitude and melodious singing talent, Srila Prabhupada gave him the title 'Raga Kumud', which means a spontaneous loving lotus. Later, Srila Prabhupada sent him to South India to preach with his senior *sannyasi* godbrothers. While he was residing in Madras, Srila Prabhupada departed from this world, and out of separation he returned to Bag Bazaar, Calcutta.

In spirit, Srila Gurudeva is always with us. Acknowledging this truth, Sripad Radharaman Das Brahmachari followed the instructions of Srila Prabhupada and started to preach extensively in India and abroad.

While on his preaching mission, there was some misconduct between the temple management board members. Radharaman Prabhu felt depressed seeing the situation and went back home to serve his family deities, Sri Sri Radha-Kishori Mohan Jiu. At that time, Srila Prabhupada appeared in his dream and ordered him to accept the renounced order (*sannyasa*). To fulfill Srila Prabhupada's order, on 12 February 1942 at Khir Chora Gopinath Ji Temple, Remuna, Odisha he took *sannyasa* initiation from his affectionate Godbrother Srila Bhakti Vichar Jajabar Goswami Maharaja. He received the name Srila Bhakti Kumud Santa Goswami Maharaja.

Thereafter he resumed preaching extensively around India, Bangladesh and different countries around Europe. His senior godbrother Srila Bhakti Vilas Tirtha Goswami Maharaja (Kunja Babu) told Srila Bhakti Kumud Santa Goswami Maharaja not to establish any temple in Mayapur. He sent his affectionate disciples to be engaged in the service of Sri Chaitanya Math (Adi-Math). Thus, Srila Santa Goswami Maharaja's initiated disciple Sripad Kanupriya Das Babaji Maharaja is currently in Adi-Math, serving as president of the present management board.

Srila Santa Goswami Maharaja established temples in many other parts of India, such as Puri (Odisha), Keshiari (Medinipore, W.B), Kargapur (Medinipur, W.B) and (Calcutta Behala, W.B). He also composed many devotional books and songs.

Presently Sripad Bhakti Vichar Bharati Maharaja, Bhakti Sundar Yati Maharaja, Bhakti Vilas Ashram Maharaja, Bhakti Prakash Madhava Maharaja and Bhakti Kamal Hrisikesh, as well as all his significant disciples, are maintaining his preaching missions.

Although Srila Santa Goswami Maharaja physically passed away in Calcutta on 7 January 2012 at 01:05, his loving service attitude for expanding Lord Chaitanya's mission is keeping him alive amongst the Gaudiya Vaishnava community. As per Srila Santa Goswami Maharaja's wish, his disciples buried (placed in *samadhi*) his holy body at Sri Gauranga Math, Keshiari, Medinipore, West Bengal.

Srila Maharaja's whole life teaches us how to practice pure devotion whilst keeping amicable relation between godbrothers and senior Vaishnavas, without any compromise even under any unavoidable circumstances.

CHAPTER FIFTEEN

Srila Bhakti Kusum Shraman Goswami Maharaja

An embodiment of tolerance, patience and equanimity appeared in Kharra village, Dhaka district, Bangladesh on Tuesday, 23 October 1900 (7 Kartik 1307) at 10:03, on the day of Giriraja Govardhan's Annakut Mahotsava, in the house of Durgacharan Das (father) and Yogamaya Devi (mother). The auspicious child was named Kanu. Since his childhood, Kanu was very studious both materially and spiritually. With the inspiration of his parents, he read the *Srimad Bhagavatam* daily. Once, Yogamaya Devi expressed how fortunate she was to have such a pious child as her own son. After hearing that, Kanu prayed to his mother to bestow blessings upon him to become a pure Vaishnava. In 1927, Kanu completed his medical degree with distinction; he also got distinctions in Sanskrit and Mathematics.

During his medical studies, Kanu was introduced to the Gaudiya Math by Bhakti Vilas Parvat Goswami Maharaja and used to visit the Madhva-Gaudiya Math situated in Dhaka. In that same year, his parents arranged his marriage. On the day of the marriage, Kanu secretly escaped from his home. He went to Bag Bazar Gaudiya Math situated in Calcutta, desiring to take initiation from Srila Prabhupada. Srila Prabhupada gave him *harinama* and *diksha* (first and second initiation) and the name Krishnakanti Das Brahmachari. Thereafter, Srila Prabhupada ordered him to go to Mayapur and offer his medical services to the devotees. Srila Prabhupada also gave him a room beside his own *bhajan kutir*.

By nature, he never hurt anyone with his words even when people spoke harshly to him. He was always seen with his chanting beads, constantly chanting the holy names with a smiling face; this was observed by anyone who came into his association. Srila Prabhupada appointed Krishnakanti Brahmachari as the publishing manager

Registered No. C ...44

দৈনিক নদীয়া-প্রকাশ

বর্ধমান-বার্ত্তাবহ

ভারতের সর্বাপেক্ষা বহুল-প্রচার—নদীয়া জেলার একমাত্র মুখপত্র

৫ম খণ্ড] সম্পাদক—প্রত্নবিদ্যালঙ্কার শ্রীপ্রমোদভূষণ চক্রবর্ত্তী [১৫১ সংখ্যা

নানাকথা

প্রায়োপবেশনের সঙ্কল্প

কংগ্রেস বুলেটিনের সম্পাদক দণ্ডিত

স্বরাজ ভবনে পুলিশ

বড়বাজারে নারীসত্যাগ্রহী ও স্বেচ্ছাসেবক গ্রেপ্তার

পুলিশের লাঠিতে মৃত্যু

জ্যাকরের আশ্বাসজনক শান্তির আশা

৩১টী বেআইনী সমিতি

পুলিশ কর্মচারীর বেশধারী এল—ইণ্ডিয়া

আবার নূতন আইন

of the *Dainik Nadia Prakash* to assist Pranavananda Das Brahmachari (later known as Srila Bhakti Pramode Puri Goswami Thakura), who was the editor. Krishnakanti Prabhu used to travel with Srila Prabhupada and serve in writing correspondence. Thus, he continued his service in expanding the mission of Lord Chaitanya under Srila Prabhupada.

Since the time of Srila Prabhupada's departure, Krishnakanti Brahmachari remained fully dedicated to serving Srila Prabhupada's mission under the guidance of Srila Bhakti Vilas Tirtha Goswami Maharaja, who was the *acharya* of Sri Chaitanya Math, Mayapur, and its branches. According to the desire of Srila Tirtha Goswami Maharaja, on the day of Gaura Purnima on 14 March 1949 (Bengali calendar: 30 Phalgun 1355), Krishnakanti Brahmachari accepted the renounced order (*sannyasa*) from him at Chaitanya Math and received the name Bhakti Kusum Shraman Goswami Maharaja.

In 1976, Srila Tirtha Goswami Maharaja physically disappeared. According to the united desire of all his godbrothers and various disciples of Srila Tirtha Goswami Maharaja, Srila Shraman Goswami Maharaja was made the *acharya* of Sri Chaitanya Math in Mayapur and its various branches. Srila Shraman Goswami Maharaja's simplicity, patience, and equanimity attracted many people from different parts of India and around the world to take shelter of him in chanting the Holy Name. During his period as *acharya* of Sri Chaitanya Math, Srila Shraman Goswami Maharaja published various books, such as Srila Prabhupada's biography, *Prema-samput, Sri Caitanyopadesa-ratnamala, Harinam-mahamantra-artha*, and so on.

Once, Srila Shraman Goswami Maharaja told one of his Bengali disciples to sweep the temple floor as it was very dirty. The devotee disobeyed his order, saying, "I am a graduate, and I am academically qualified. Did I join the temple to sweep the floor?" Srila Shraman Goswami Maharaja simply smiled and continued chanting the Hare Krishna *maha-mantra* on his beads. Twenty years later, a devotee found that same *brahmachari* lamenting while sweeping the floor of Howrah Railway Station in West Bengal. This incident teaches us that if we ignore a pure devotee's desire, then the Lord forces us into a worse condition.

At the age of 86, on 11 December 1986, the day of Moksada Ekadasi Gita Jayanti, when everyone was reading the *Bhagavad Gita* (a book that represents complete self-surrender and contains the direct words of Bhagavan Sri Krishna), Srila Shraman Goswami Maharaja physically passed away with a smiling face while chanting the Hare Krishna *maha-mantra* at Chaitanya Math, Mayapur. His *samadhi* is in his *bhajan kutir* adjacent to Srila Prabhupada's *bhajan kutir* at Adi-math Sri Chaitanya Math. Srila Shraman Goswami Maharaja's life teaches us that in this age of hypocrisy and quarrel, we need to keep patience in order to successfully continue our spiritual practice in every aspect.

CHAPTER SIXTEEN

SRILA BHAKTI MAYUKH BHAGAVAT GOSWAMI MAHARAJA

According to the *sastra*, we know that Baladeva is the manifestation of Lord Krishna. That same Lord Baladeva appeared in this world, during this age of turmoil, in the form of Nityananda Prabhu on the 13th day of the waxing moon in the month of Phalguna. On that same day, in the year 1904 (Bengali year 1311, Phalguna), Bhakti Mayukh Bhagavat Goswami, a spiritual descendant of Lord Nityananda, appeared in a reputed family in the village of Chinpay, Birbhum district, West Bengal. His father was Sriyukta Rama Kumar Mukhopadhyay, and his mother, Srimati Kusum Kamini Devi. Since his childhood, Srila Bhagavat Goswami Maharaja was naturally truthful, possessed sound character and was charismatic. Therefore, all the villagers had great affection and respect for him.

As he grew older, his eagerness to realize divine love for the Supreme Lord increased. He sat in a solitary place, his eyes filled with tears, and desired to come into contact with a genuine spiritual master. The Supreme Lord always fulfils the desires of his devotees. One day, he had a dream wherein he saw His Divine Grace Srila Prabhupada. Srila Bhagavat Goswami Maharaja did not know who Srila Prabhupada was but realized that the person he had seen in his dream was certainly his worshipful *guru*. From that time onward, he was anxious to meet the great personality he had seen in his dream. By the mercy of the Lord, Srila Bhagavat Maharaja met that personality on Gaura Purnima day. On that same day, although he was not listed for initiation, nevertheless, Srila Bhagavat Maharaja shaved his head and eagerly waited to get *harinama* initiation from Srila Prabhupada. Out of his causeless mercy, Srila Prabhupada gave him *harinama* initiation and told all surrounding devotees, "All of you may not know him, but I know him from before." Although this was the first time that Srila Bhagavat

Maharaja was physically meeting Srila Prabhupada, Srila Prabhupada expressed to all the devotees that he knew Srila Bhagavat Maharaja from before.

Within one year, he left his family life and dedicated his whole life to the service of his *gurudeva*. In a short period of time, Srila Prabhupada gave him second initiation (*diksha*), and he got the spiritual name Shubhavilasa Dasa Adhikari. After second initiation, Srila Prabhupada appointed Shubhavilasa Prabhu as a teacher of *dharma* in the Bhaktivinoda Institute at Mayapur. Soon, Srila Prabhupada appointed him as the main editor of the *Dainik Nadia Prakash* daily spiritual newsletter. He efficiently wrote and proofread articles and managed the press. Srila Prabhupada saw Shubhavilasa Prabhu's dedication in publication service and gave him the title 'Bhakti-mayukh,' meaning one who has prime devotion. Eventually, Srila Prabhupada made him a *Mahopadeshaka* on Gaura Purnima 1936, meaning that he was a great devotional advisor.

In 1948, on Srila Prabhupada's Vyasa Puja, Srila Bhakti Bhudev Srauti Goswami Maharaja bestowed the order of *sannyasa* upon Shubhavilasa Prabhu in Jhargrama, Medinipur, West Bengal in the Gaura Sarasvata Math. Shubhavilasa Prabhu received the name Tridandi Swami Bhakti Mayukh Bhagavat Goswami Maharaja. Although he had the inner desire to live in Vrindavan and spend the rest of his life in solitary devotional practice, Srila Bhagavat Goswami Maharaja eventually established his first preaching center at his birthplace in 1951. In 1971, Srila Bhagavat Goswami Maharaja established another preaching center at Bolpur, Shantiniketan, West Bengal. In 1986, he established another preaching center in the city of Purulia, West Bengal. All his godbrothers were pleased to see his firm faith in *guru*, his commitment in serving Sri Hari, Guru and Vaishnavas, his enthusiasm in chanting the Hare Krishna *maha-mantra* and his one-pointed surrender.

Seeing his devotional qualities, many pious people took shelter of him and engaged in their devotional practice. Srila Bhagavat Goswami Maharaja wrote many articles for the monthly *Chaitanya Vani* magazine published by Sri Chaitanya Gaudiya Math. He also compiled Srila Prabhupada's *harikatha* and published an extremely attractive book called *Srila Prabhupader Upadesamrta – The nectarine teachings of Srila Prabhupada.*

On Sunday, 28 December 1986 at 09:05 (Bengali calendar – 12 Poush 1393 Sukla Dvadasi 12th day of waxing-moon cycle), at the age of 82, Srila Bhagavat Goswami Maharaja left this world from his room located in his temple at Raipur, Birbhum district while remembering the mid-day pastimes of Sri Sri Radha Govinda, which take place in Radhakunda (*madhyahna-lila*). Srila Bhagavat Goswami Maharaja's entire life teaches us to wholeheartedly dedicate ourselves to Sri Hari, Guru and Vaishnavas. This is the only way to reach our spiritual goal, which is to become eternal servants of the Divine Couple, Sri Sri Radha Krishna. Srila Bhagavat Goswami Maharaja was a shining example of a pure, unparalleled, divine personality.

SRILA BHAKTI PRADIP TIRTHA GOSWAMI MAHARAJA

According to Vaishnava scriptures, the absolute truth of *guru-tattva* is that Sri Guru is one without a second. During spring in 1876 (Bangla 1283, in the month of Chaitra), Lord Chaitanya brought one of his significant spiritual descendants, Srila Bhakti Pradip Tirtha Goswami Maharaja, into this world as the son of Rajani Kanta Basu and Srimati Vidhumukhi Devi. Born in the village of Sandeep Hatia, district Noyakhali, Bangladesh, the baby boy was named Sri Jagadish Chandra Basu. Since his childhood, he was extraordinarily talented in every aspect, academically and spiritually. He obtained a B.A. degree from Calcutta University and worked as a high school teacher.

On 25 March 1910, at the age of 34, Sri Jagadish Chandra had the opportunity to meet with Srila Bhaktivinoda Thakura, the reviver of Lord Chaitanya's pure devotional path. Seeing Jagadish Chandra's intelligence, humility and simplicity, within a short period of time Srila Bhaktivinoda Thakura gave him initiation. After the initiation ceremony, Srila Bhaktivinoda Thakura instructed him to spread the loving message of Lord Chaitanya both locally and internationally. At the time, he was unable to follow the instruction due to being bound in household life.

Once his wife physically expired, his goal was to fulfill his *gurudeva*'s instruction to spread the loving message of Lord Chaitanya. In 1910, he met Srila Bimala Prasad, who was later known as Srila Prabhupada.

On 23 June 1914, Bhaktivinoda Thakura physically disappeared from this world while in Calcutta. However, before leaving this world, Bhaktivinoda Thakura again gave Sri Jagadish Chandra the same instruction, to spread the loving message of Lord Chaitanya globally. On 1 November 1920, Sri Jagadish Chandra was given *sannyasa* initiation by Srila Prabhupada and received the name

Bhakti Pradip Tirtha Goswami Maharaja. Thereafter, as per Srila Prabhupada's instructions, he translated the *Bhagavad Gita* into the English language while publishing many other books. His spiritual talent was extremely attractive, and he eventually received different spiritual titles from Srila Prabhupada, such as '*Vidya Vinod*', '*Bhakti Shastri*' and '*Sampradaya Vaibhav Acharya*'.

On 18 March 1933, in order to fulfill the final instructions of Bhaktivinoda Thakura, Srila Prabhupada sent Srila Bhakti Pradip Tirtha Goswami Maharaja to Europe along with Srila Bhakti Hridaya Bon Goswami Maharaja and Sri Samvidananda Das Prabhu.

In 1943, at the age of 67, Srila Bhakti Pradip Tirtha Goswami Maharaja decided to perform solitary *bhajan* at Purusottam Math in Sri Jagannath Puri Dham. Due to some unavoidable circumstances, Bhakti Pradip Tirtha Goswami Maharaja served as *acharya* of the Gaudiya Mission for last two years of his life. On the auspicious full-moon day (Purnima) in the month of Agrahayana (Nov-Dec) in 1954, Bhakti Pradip Tirtha Goswami Maharaja physically left us. In spirit, he is eternally teaching us Vaishnava etiquette, such as simplicity, generosity, humility, tolerance, divinity, being free from material recognition and offering due respect to everyone. Through chanting the Hare Krishna *maha-mantra*, these qualities will manifest in our *chitta* (consciousness, intelligence, heart and mind), which will allow us to reach the ultimate goal of divinity.

SRILA BHAKTI PRAJNAN KESHAVA GOSWAMI MAHARAJA

His Divine Grace Srila Bhakti Prajnan Keshava Goswami Maharaja appeared on the auspicious day of *tritiya tithi* on 24 January 1898 in the village of Banari Para, in the district of Barisal near Jessore, Bangladesh. He was born in the famous Guha dynasty in a wealthy and prominent *zamindar* family. His father was Sri Sarat Candra Guha, a Vaishnava, and his chaste and devoted mother was Bhuvana Mohini Devi. His name at birth was Sri Vinode Bihari.

In his childhood, he was very intelligent and introspective; he possessed an excellent character and above all was naturally spiritually minded. He was educated in Sanskrit and *Vedanta* at an early age, and from his father's library he had read *Bhagavad-Gita, Srimad Bhagavatam* and *Sri Chaitanya-charitamrita* even before he went to university, where he excelled in his studies.

In 1915, he met Srila Prabhupada and at the age of 17 was given first initiation *(harinama)*. Four years later in 1919, Srila Prabhupada gave him second initiation *(diksha)*, along with the responsibility as managing editor of the *Gaudiya* periodical in Krishnanagar. In addition to editing the periodical, he regularly contributed many articles on Vaishnava philosophy.

Srila Prabhupada gave him the title 'Kriti-ratna' due to his unsurpassed zeal in serving Sri Guru and Vaishnavas. Once, he heard Srila Prabhupada mention that he had not acquired Srila Saccidananda Bhaktivinoda Thakura's *bhajan kutir* in Godruma. Taking that as a direct order from his *guru*, he went to Godruma and was successful in securing that *bhajan kutir* for the Gaudiya Math.

As is well known, Srila Prabhupada introduced *nama-sankirtan* and massive circumambulation *(parikrama)* of the nine islands of Sri Navadwip Dham annually from 1920 onwards. The deities were mounted upon an elephant in a magnificent and grand style amidst a horde of devotees and pilgrims all performing *kirtan* with 108 *mridanga* players along with horns, kettledrums and *karatals*. The thunderous and jubilant sound of *kirtan* could be heard for miles. In March 1925, while performing *parikrama* on the island of Sri Koladwip, the *parikrama* party was viciously attacked by an organized assault of malicious and evil-minded miscreants. All the pilgrims and devotees began to flee for their lives. There was such a flurry of bricks and stones that Srila Prabhupada's very life was in jeopardy and great danger.

Understanding the utmost gravity of the situation, Vinode Bihari Brahmachari quickly took his *guru* into a doorway and resourcefully interchanged his *brahmachari* garments with Srila Prabhupada's *sannyasa* cloth and disguised him. Not knowing whether they would survive, when Vinode Bihari Brahmachari was putting on his *guru's sannyasa* cloth, Srila Prabhupada spontaneously gave Vinode Bihari Brahmachari the *sannyasa mantra* and initiated him into the *ashram* of *sannyasa*. Then, the disciple, protecting his *guru*, took Srila Prabhupada courageously to safety.

In Srila Bhakti Prajnan Keshava Goswami Maharaja's *pranam mantra*, the word *simha,* meaning lion, glorifies his fearless courage for saving Srila Prabhupada's life.

namo oṁ viṣṇupādāya ācārya-siṁha-rūpine
śrī-śrīmad bhakti-prajñana keśava iti nāmine

"I offer my obeisance to Srila Bhakti Prajnan Keshava Goswami Maharaja, the lion-like *acharya* who never fears, having taken shelter of the Supreme Lord's lotus feet."

Once, there was a court case regarding the Srivas Angan land. Some Muslims complained that the land was their own land for a graveyard. However, in order to prove that that was not the case, Vinoda Da planted many trees, roses, and *tulasi* plants and made a beautiful garden overnight. When the inspectors came the next day to inspect and find out the facts, they saw the garden and could not believe that the same land which was claimed by the Muslims to be a graveyard was actually a beautiful garden. Vinoda Da was so intelligent ,and in this way he secured the Srivas Angan land, which is the *nitya-sankirtana rasa-sthali*.

Whenever Vinoda Da crossed the river Ganga, he would just put his hand into his pocket and give whatever money he had to the boatman. People complained to Srila Prabhupada that he was unnecessarily spending money. Then Srila Prabhupada said, "How much was your daily expense when you were a householder?" They replied saying two *rupees*, three *rupees*, etc. Then Srila Prabhupada asked, "Now how much do you all spend?" Then, they replied four or five *rupees*. So, they were spending more. Then Srila Prabhupada said, "When Vinoda Da was a householder, his daily expense was 100 *rupees*, and he now spends 10 *rupees*." Srila Prabhupada knew that Vinoda Da was spending money like that for the boat so that the local people would be in favor of the Gaudiya Maths. This was his long-term vision.

There is yet another incident connected to his saving Srila Prabhupada that must be revealed. Seeing the spiritually wretched, deplorable condition of the people of Navadwip, Srila Prabhupada, feeling compassion, was determined to redeem them all. So, during the evening spiritual discourses (*harikatha satsang*), he requested which one of his disciples would take the responsibility to build a temple in Navadwip and deliver the sinners there. Not even a pin drop could be heard in the hall. Seeing that no one was willing to step up and satisfy Srila Prabhupada's desire, Vinoda Da stood up and said he would take the responsibility to build a temple to redeem the people of Navadwip, and this manifested magnificently as Sri Devananda Gaudiya Math.

In the year 1929, Srila Prabupada was extremely pleased by Vinode Bihari Brahmachari's lectures on devotion, his preaching and his writing of the famous book *Vaishnava Vijaya Mayavadi Jivani (The Victory of Vaishnavasim and the Life History of Mayavadism)*. He entrusted Vinoda Da to take care of the thousands of Vedic books in his library.

Vinode Bihari Brahmachari used to teach that the Supreme Lord Krishna is attained through *harinama* (His transcendental name), which reaches our hearts exclusively through the purified ear and not through the defective and deceptive organ of the eye.

After Srila Prabhupada's departure in 1937, Vinode Bihari Brahmachari mourned the disappearance of his *gurudeva* bitterly. Resolute with great faith, he powerfully preached *sanatana dharma, bhagavat dharma* and the message of Sri Chaitanya Mahaprabhu everywhere he went.

In 1941 on Gaura Purnima day, in Katwa, where Sri Krishna Chaitanya Mahaprabhu had received *sannyasa*, Vinode Bihari Brahmachari formally accepted *sannyasa* from Srila Bhakti Rakshak Sridhar Dev Goswami Maharaja. Srila Bhakti Pramode Puri Goswami Maharaja was the priest who conducted the fire sacrifice. At that time, Vinode Bihari Brahmachari received the name Srila Bhakti Prajnan Keshava Maharaja.

Later that same year, he established Sri Gaudiya Vedanta Samiti registered in Calcutta. In 1942, he established Sri Devananda Gaudiya Math at Koladwip in Sri Navadwip Dham and thereafter established 37 temples across India. On 13 December 1954, he founded Sri Keshavaji Gaudiya Math in Mathura. On 17 September 1959, at Sri Keshavaji Gaudiya Math in Mathura, Srila Bhakti Prajnan Keshava Goswami Maharaja initiated Srila A.C. Bhaktivedanta Swami into the *ashram* of *sannyasa*. Srila Bhaktivedanta Swami Maharaja would later go to the United States and establish the International Society for Krishna Consciousness (ISKCON), which would fulfill Sri Chaitanya Mahaprabhu's prophecy that the holy names of Krishna would be sung in every town, city and village on Earth.

Srila Keshava Goswami Maharaja appointed Srila Bhaktivedanta Vaman Goswami Maharaja as the successor to his mission. Srila Vaman Goswami Maharaja had received *harinama* initiation from Srila Prabhupada at the age of 9 in 1930. He knew, from memory, hundreds of *shlokas* and was knowledgeable of all *tattvas* and *siddhanta*. He was unique in that he was the only *diksha* disciple of Srila Bhakti Prajnan Keshava Goswami Maharaja who was his godbrother, his very first disciple and a founding member of Sri Gaudiya Vedanta Samiti as well.

During *chaturmasya vrata* in 1968, Srila Keshava Goswami Maharaja announced to his disciples that they should all join him as he would be leaving his body in the month of Kartik. On Kartik Purnima night, 6 October 1968, at Sri Devananda Gaudiya Math in Sri Koladwip, Sri Navadwip Dham, Srila Keshava Goswami Maharaja entered into the *aprakata-lila* in his original *svarupa* as Vinoda Manjari, joining his *gurudeva*, Srila Prabhupada, in his original *svarupa* as Nayanamani Manjari − both eternal servitors of Sri Rupa Manjari and Sri Sri Radha Krishna in Goloka Vrindavan.

CHAPTER NINETEEN

SRILA BHAKTI PRAKASH ARANYA GOSWAMI MAHARAJA

One of Srila Prabhupada's spiritual descendants is Srila Bhakti Prakash Aranya Goswami Maharaja. He was born in the village of Gangarampur, Jessore, Bangladesh in 1887. His parents named him Yadunath, which means Lord of the Yadava dynasty. Since his childhood, he had spontaneous attachment for Radha-Krishna's services. Due to family tradition and pressure, he married, but by the Lords' desire he had no children.

Although Yadunath faced many obstacles in his family life, he never left his service mood. Yadunath ran a shop in his village. Once, Srila Prabhupada came to Yadunath's village area with his preaching team. The local people arranged a public program with Srila Prabhupada's discourses and Mahajan Padavali *kirtans*. After the programs, Yadunath came to see Srila Prabhupada personally. At that time, Srila Prabhupada gave him the instruction to engage in the service of Lord Hari to his best ability. After hearing Srila Prabhupada's instruction, Yadunath immediately decided to leave his shop and home, and came with Srila Prabhupada to Bag Bazar Gaudiya Math, Calcutta.

Srila Prabhupada noticed his skill for spreading the loving message of Lord Chaitanya and his sound knowledge of the different *shastras*. He was always preaching at universities and to educated persons like professors. All of them were impressed hearing his philosophical explanation. He was also skilled in publicizing various devotional books and magazines. Seeing this, Srila Prabhupada was very happy and bestowed his mercy upon him. Srila Aranya Maharaja's discourses were replicas of Srila Prabhupada's words. After Srila Prabhupada's physical departure, Srila Aranya Maharaja spent most of the time in Calcutta at the Sri Chaitanya Gaudiya Math temple of his godbrother Srila Bhakti Dayita Madhava Goswami Maharaja. Srila Aranya Maharaja had lots of enthusiasm for preaching and used to travel with his godbrothers and other *brahmacharis*. He used to perform the Vrindavan Dham and Navadwip Dhama *parikramas* barefoot.

Once, Srila Aranya Goswami Maharaja had finished his preaching tour in Bangladesh and was crossing the Padma River by boat. As they were in the middle of the river, a huge storm arrived. The boatman said, "O *sadhu*! We are in trouble. We will not be able to survive the storm." Srila Aranya Maharaja stood up holding his *sannyasa danda* and started crying and chanting, "Jaya Prabhupada! Jaya Prabhupada! Jaya Prabhupada!" At that time, Srila Prabhupada was at Bag Bazar Gaudiya Math. He called all the *brahmacharis* and told them, "Everyone should chant *kirtan*. Aranya Maharaja is in trouble." Everyone started chanting along with Srila Prabhupada. Meanwhile, the huge storm began to calm down at the Padma River. Seeing this, the boatman fell at the feet of Aranya Maharaja; he was crying and said, "O *sadhu*! By your mercy, today I have survived, the boat has survived and the other people traveling on this boat have survived.

Before his physical departure, he manifest illness pastimes for two months at Sri Chaitanya Gaudiya Math, Vrindavan. After that, he came to Bengal for preaching and travelled with his godbrothers. On Friday, 6 January 1967 (Ekadasi day) at 18:30 in the house of Nani Gopal Kundu, located in Dhalchita, Basirhat, 24 Parganas, West Bengal, at the age of 80, whilst chanting the verse *tava kathāmṛtam tapta jīvanam*, he left his body. He was surrounded by godbrothers and disciples. Maharaja's exemplary preaching enthusiasm, austerity, adjustment with all devotees (including his godbrothers, disciples and householders) and his attentive listening to his *gurudeva*'s discourses, which he later repeated (as is), are our inspiration for following in the footsteps of Sri Guru and Vaishnavas. If anyone reads his life history, he will definitely get pure devotion by following in the footsteps of the spiritual master and the Vaishnavas, which is the main goal of spiritual practice.

CHAPTER TWENTY

SRILA BHAKTI PRAMODE PURI GOSWAMI MAHARAJA

During autumn in Bengal, amidst Navaratri Durga Puja celebrations, the clouds were blissfully moving about in the sky. Out of bliss, Indradeva was sprinkling rain from time to time, creating a cool atmosphere. The penetrating sounds of the traditional Bengali drums (*dhaak*) were resounding through the environment in the festive mood of Durga Puja. It seemed like the autumn season, Durga Devi and the king of heaven, Indradeva, were happily welcoming a spiritually significant baby boy. He was born in the early hours of the morning on Wednesday, 19 October 1898 (4th day of the waxing-moon cycle of the Navaratri festival, Gaura Chaturdashi). The baby appeared in a rigid Chakravarti *brahmana* family on the banks of the Kapotaksha River in Ganganandapur village, Jessore District, Bangladesh. The father, Tarinicharan Chakravarti, and the mother, Ramrangini Devi, named their baby Pramode Bhushan Chakravarti.

Tarinicharan was a schoolteacher. He was not so financially well off, so his wife, Ramrangini Devi, began to run a *goshala*, taking care of cows and selling milk. One day, when Pramode Bhushan was around six or seven years old, he was assisting his mother in the *goshala* when he noticed that his mother was discriminating between the cows: giving straw, mustard cakes, sesame cakes, jaggery and other nutritious foods to some cows and giving mediocre food to the other cows. Out of curiosity, he asked his mother why she was acting in this way. His mother said, "I am giving the good food to the cows who are providing us with milk and not to the ones who do not give us milk." Immediately, the young Pramode Bhushan said, "I am not benefitting you in any way. Rather, you are forced to spend lots of money on maintaining me. So why are you giving me good food? From today onwards, please treat me as you are treating the cows who don't give milk."

One day, Ramrangini Devi was preparing to cook a fish, which was still alive and writhing in severe pain. At that time, Pramode Bhushan had just arrived home from school and witnessed the agony of the fish, which brought tears to his eyes. His mother thought, "Today, my son must have quarreled with his classmates at school." To pacify him, she began to speak in an affectionate tone. "Has anything happened to you today? Did someone scold you? Tell me, who has told you what? Speak to me, my dear child." With tears in his eyes, Pramode Bhushan replied, "Mother, why are you not chopping me into pieces and cooking me? I am also helpless like that fish. How can you clean this bloody fish, cook it and then eat it? If you ever bring fish into this kitchen, I will never eat anything cooked here again. This is my final resolution." Hearing these intelligent words of the small boy, Mother Ramrangini Devi became struck with wonder. From that day onwards, no fish was ever brought into or cooked in the kitchen. Pramode Bhushan had empathy and compassion for all living beings since his childhood.

While living in Ganganandapur, Pramode Bhushan had the association of his neighbor Bhaktiratna Thakura, who was a godbrother of Bhaktivinoda Thakura. Due to his compassionate nature towards all living beings, Pramode Bhushan received much affection from Bhaktiratna Thakura and was engaged in the service of Bhaktiratna Thakura's personal deities, Sri Sri Radha Madanamohana. During his services to Sri Sri Radha Madanamohana, Pramode Bhushan had the opportunity of seeing Bhaktivinoda Thakura when the latter visited Bhaktiratna Thakura. In 1915, being inspired by Bhaktiratna Thakura, Pramode Bhushan made his first visit to Mayapur to see Bimala Prasad.

One winter night, during his service to Sri Sri Radha Madanamohana, Pramode Bhushan accidentally forgot

to offer Madanamohana a blanket before putting Him to rest. Pramode Bhushan suffered the entire night due to the cold weather in his own house and was afflicted by a fever. Furthermore, on that very night, Madanamohana complained to Bhaktiratna Thakura, saying, "I am suffering from cold now." Early the next morning, Pramode Bhushan went to the Madanamohana temple while still in a feverish state. There, he met Bhaktiratna Thakura, who, without paying any attention to his physical distress, immediately told him, "Take a bath in the cold pond and offer a blanket to Madanamohana. That will relieve you of your ailment." Pramode Bhushan followed the instructions and as a result, he was relieved of the distress born of the fever and cold, and he felt genuine bliss. Before his initiation, Pramode Bhushan was already experiencing direct reciprocations with the deities of the Lord.

Pramode Bhushan initially studied in his village's school. He then completed his high school in Baruipur, located in the 24-parganas near Calcutta, and completed his honors degree in Chemistry from Bangavasi College, Calcutta. He was then employed as a port officer.

Pramode Bhushan regularly attended Bimala Prasad's spiritual discourses in the evening after work, at the Ultadingi Junction Gaudiya Math. One day, Pramode Bhushan returned home from his office to his rented room and changed his clothes. He was putting on his shoes to leave for the evening lecture when suddenly a scorpion, which was hiding inside the shoes, stung him. Pramode Bhushan's attraction for hearing Srila Prabhupada's discourses was so great that even the severe pain of the bite could not keep him confined at home. He rushed to the *math*. There, the transcendental mellows of Srila Prabhupada's lecture made him forget about the pain of the scorpion bite, but the moment the discourse was over,

he began to feel severe pain. At the end of his recitation, Srila Prabhupada, being omniscient, said to Pramode Bhushan, "It seems that something has happened to you." Pramode Bhushan narrated the whole incident, to which Srila Prabhupada replied, "Your eagerness to hear the discourses while ignoring the scorpion sting has certainly amazed me. From today onwards, you should try to attend your office while staying in the *math*." Pramode Bhushan took these words to heart and happily returned to his rented room, paying no heed to the severe pain he was experiencing.

Pramode Bhushan began staying at the *math* while continuing to work. Two years later, at the age of 23, Pramode Bhushan received *harinama* (first initiation), *diksha* (second initiation) and saffron cloth on Janmashtami from Srila Prabhupada. He was thereafter known as Pranavananda Brahmachari and became a full-time member of the Gaudiya Math. Srila Prabhupada gave Pranavananda a pen and engaged him to take dictation from Srila Prabhupada and serve as editor of the daily spiritual newsletter, *Dainik Nadia Prakash*. Since Pranavananda was so dedicated to Srila Prabhupada, he was engaged as a *kirtaniya, pujari* and personal servant of Srila Prabhupada. From 1923 to 1936, Srila Prabhupada kept Pranavananda, whom he lovingly called, Pranava, near to him as much as possible.

After Srila Prabhupada's physical departure, Pranavananda left Bag Bazar Gaudiya Math and stayed with his godbrothers Bhakti Hridaya Bon Goswami Maharaja and Akinchan Krishnadas Babaji Maharaja in a rented apartment in Tollygunge, Calcutta. One day before sunrise, a widow appeared at the doorstep of the apartment and was asking for Pranavananda. Pranavananda had opened the door and was surprised to see this widow looking for him as he did not even know

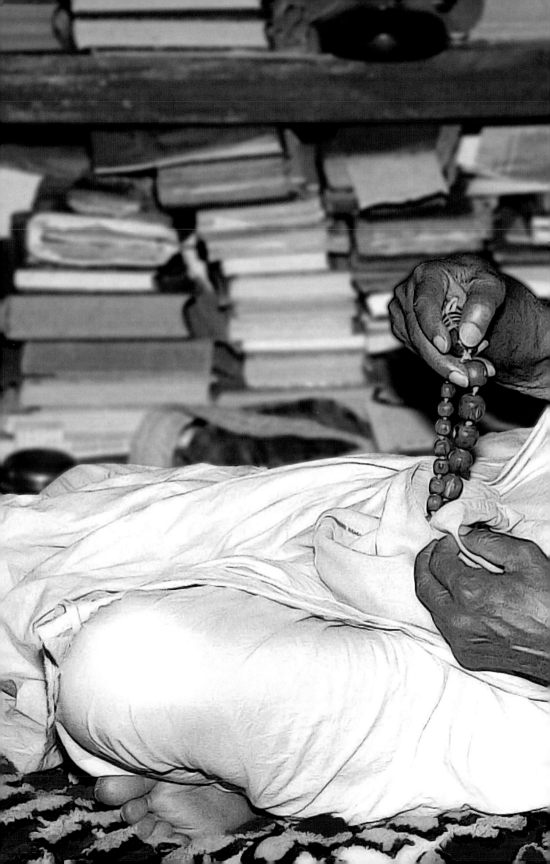

who she was. The widow explained, "I had these deities of Radha-Krishna at home but was not worshiping Them. Last night, Radha-Krishna came in my dream and told me to bring Them to you at this very address. Please accept these deities from me. Otherwise, my whole family will be destroyed; this is what I was told in my dream." Pranavananda happily accepted the deities. His mother used to worship Sri Sri Radha-Gopinath deities at her home. Due to his attachment to his mother and her deities, he named these newly received deities Sri Sri Radha-Gopinath.

Thereafter, according to the request of his senior godbrother Kunjabihari Vidyabhushan (later known as Srila Bhakti Vilas Tirtha Goswami Maharaja), Pranavananda became the temple in-charge and *pujari* at Lord Chaitanya's birthplace, Yogapith temple, Mayapur. He also served as the editor of the *Gaudiya* magazine. One night, Srila Prabhupada appeared in Pranavananda's dream and initiated him with the *sannyasa mantra*. The next morning, he wrote down the *mantra* in his diary. On 3 March 1947, the Ekadasi *tithi* preceding Gaura Purnima, Pranavananda formally took *sannyasa* at the Gaura Gadadhar temple in Champahati from his very dear godbrother Srila Bhakti Gaurav Vaikhanas Goswami Maharaja and received the name Srila Bhakti Pramode Puri Goswami Maharaja (Srila Puri Goswami Maharaja). For over eight years, until 1955, Srila Puri Goswami Maharaja continued serving at the Yogapith temple.

Due to some unforeseen circumstances, Srila Puri Goswami Maharaja moved to the banks of the Ganga at Kalna (*khati-ganga*) in April 1955 (1 Vaishakh 1362) where he lived for three years, engaging in intense spiritual practice. In 1958, on the day of Radhashtami, the king of Burdwan district gave Srila Puri Goswami Maharaja the ancient temple of Ananta Basudeva located in Kalna. In 1961, Srila Bhakti Dayita Madhava Goswami Maharaja requested Srila Puri Goswami Maharaja to look after the publication department of Sri Chaitanya Gaudiya Math. In accordance with his godbrother's request, Srila Puri Goswami Maharaja handed over the responsibilities of the Ananta Basudeva temple to his brother, Nanigopal, and shifted to Sri Chaitanya Gaudiya Math to serve as the chief editor of the *Chaitanya Vani* magazine and as the head of all publications of the institution.

Through the will of the Lord, Srila Puri Goswami Maharaja established Sri Gopinath Gaudiya Math in Mayapur in 1987. In just a short period of time, many centers manifested throughout India at Medinipur, Calcutta, Jagannath Puri and Vrindavan. Although he was at a very advanced age, Srila Puri Goswami Maharaja established perfect deity worship, goshalas, spiritual publications and so on in Sri Gopinath Gaudiya Math. He gave shelter to many spiritual seekers.

Srila Puri Goswami Maharaja was very much attached to Gadadhar Pandit. Therefore, he established the deities of Sri Sri Gaura Gadadhar in the Mayapur temple. One hot summer afternoon, Srila Puri Goswami Maharaja suddenly told the temple manager to immediately call for the *pujari* who was serving the deities in the temple room. When the *pujari* entered his *bhajan kutir*, Srila Puri Goswami Maharaja gravely exclaimed, "Why did you hit Gadadhar with your elbow? You better beg for forgiveness; otherwise, you will be entangled in material life very, very soon." As soon as the *pujari* left the room, the temple manager, who was standing by the side of Srila Puri Goswami Maharaja, spoke, "Guru Maharaja, how did you know that the *pujari* hit Gadadhar Pandit? The temple room has no windows, and the doors were completely closed." Srila Puri Goswami Maharaja

replied, "Baba, Gadadhar Pandit personally came here to me in my room and complained to me, saying that the *pujari* had hit Him and misbehaved with Him." Such was the intense meditation and perfection in deity worship that Srila Puri Goswami Maharaja exhibited.

In 1997, Srila Puri Goswami Maharaja wrote his will and his successor. Following in the footsteps of his dearmost Gadadhar Pandit, Srila Puri Goswami Maharaja expressed his desire to take *kshetra-sannyasa* in Jagannath Puri Dham and live there permanently until the time of leaving his body.

At 02:10 on Monday 22 November 1999, in his *bhajan kutir* at Sri Gopinath Gaudiya Math's branch located in Jagannath Puri Dham, Srila Puri Goswami Maharaja physically departed from this world. Prior to leaving his body, he had said, "Since my *gurudeva*, Srila Prabhupada Bhaktisiddhanta Saraswati Goswami Thakura, *parama-gurudeva*, Srila Gaura Kishore Das Babaji Maharaja, and godbrothers are all in *samadhi* in Mayapur, I would also like to be put into *samadhi* there after leaving my body." According to his will, his body was brought to Mayapur and put into *samadhi* in the premises of his temple.

Srila Puri Goswami Maharaja's entire life shows the example of serving the *guru parampara* with full sincerity, purity, humility and tolerance. He was the embodiment of the third verse of the *Shiksastakam*:

tṛṇād api sunīcena taror api sahiṣṇunā
amāninā mānadena kīrtanīyaḥ sadā hariḥ

His eternal identity in Goloka Vrindavan is Sri Palash Manjari, who picks flowers for the service of Sri Sri Radha-Gopinath.

CHAPTER TWENTY-ONE

SRILA BHAKTI RAKSHAK SRIDHAR GOSWAMI MAHARAJA

representative of Srila Rupa Goswami, who propagated pure love, appeared as a ray from the divine lotus feet of Sri Krishna Chaitanya Mahaprabhu. This representative of the Supreme Lord appeared in Hapaniya, Burdwan district, West Bengal in a Bhattacharya *brahmana* family on 10 October 1895 (Bengali calendar: 26 Ashwin 1302). He was the son of Upendra Chandra Deva Sharma Bhattacharya Vidyaratna and Srimati Gauri Bala Devi, who named the baby Ramendra Sundar Bhattacharya. His father was a famous scholar who was known as 'Vidyaratna' (jewel of knowledge). Ramendra Sundar was as studious as his father and excelled in his primary and secondary school studies. He qualified with a B.A. degree in law and became connected with M. K. Gandhi's non-cooperation movement, fighting for Indian independence from British rule.

In 1923, Lord Sri Krishna Chaitanya Mahaprabhu miraculously pulled Ramendra Sundar to His movement. One day, Ramendra Sundar was drawn to Srila Prabhupada's first Gaudiya Math on Ultadingi Junction Road. When he entered the *math*, Pranavananda Das Brahmachari was giving a discourse on the *Srimad Bhagavatam*. Every day, after Pranavananda's class, Srila Prabhupada would also give discourse on the *Srimad Bhagavatam*. Ramendra Sundar listened attentively and began to attend the discourses on a daily basis. At that time, Srila Prabhupada's secretary, Kunjabihari Vidyabhushan Prabhu, doubting that Ramendra Sundar was a spy of the British government, engaged Pranavananda Das Brahmachari to investigate Ramendra Sundar. After three days of investigation, Pranavananda Das Brahmachari dismissed the concern, saying that Ramendra Sundar would be an asset to the *sampradaya*.

In 1926, Srila Prabhupada mercifully gave him *harinama* (first initiation). A few months later, Srila Prabhupada gave him *diksha* (second initiation) and the name Ramananda Prabhu. Ramananda wholeheartedly engaged himself in serving Srila Prabhupada's mission. All his godbrothers and even Srila Prabhupada were astonished to see Ramananda's writing skill in the Sanskrit language. Srila Prabhupada gave him the title 'Sastra Nipuna', which means he who is expertly skilled in all scriptures. In 1930, Srila Prabhupada gave Ramananda *sannyasa* initiation along with the new name Bhakti Rakshak Sridhar Goswami Maharaja.

Srila Prabhupada engaged Srila Sridhar Goswami Maharaja in preaching. Whenever any problems arose in the preaching field, Srila Prabhupada would send Srila Sridhar Goswami Maharaja to solve the problem. In this regard, I would like to relate an incident. In Bangladesh, Siddhasvarupa Prabhu (later known as Srila Bhakti Srirupa Siddhanti Goswami Maharaja), Srila Bhakti Rakshak Sridhar Goswami Maharaja and Hayagriva Brahmachari (later known as Srila Bhakti Dayita Madhava Goswami Maharaja) were busy preaching to the masses. In one program, Siddhasvarupa Prabhu passed a negative opinion about a famous religious institution in Bengal known as the Ramakrishna Mission. The entire audience opposed him. The next day, on the same stage, Srila Sridhar Goswami Maharaja explained about how the scriptures say that Shankaracharya spread *mayavada* (the philosophy of impersonalism). He said, "The scriptures say that Shankaracharya preached impersonalism, which is in and of itself not the genuine message of the Lord. Shankaracharya is an incarnation of Lord Shiva, but the scriptures themselves state that he preached an incorrect philosophy. Therefore, how can we even consider that the philosophy of Ramakrishna

Mission is genuine and not impersonalism?" After this logical explanation, the members of the audience understood a whole new dimension of the scriptures and became favorable towards the Gaudiya Math and Gaudiya Vaishnavism.

Once, in the Theological Society in Chennai, Tamil Nadu, Srila Sridhar Goswami Maharaja was giving a discourse. He was allotted 15 minutes to speak. He said, "We cannot serve Krishna. We cannot see Krishna. We cannot be with Krishna." In this way, he spoke for 15 minutes. After his discourse, a lawyer asked him some questions. "If we are not able to see Krishna and serve Krishna, then why should we waste our time in trying to serve Him?" In reply, Srila Sridhar Goswami Maharaja said, "We can see Krishna and we can serve Krishna." Then, the lawyer said, "This is our job. This is how we, lawyers, speak. We can make 'yes' into 'no' and we can make 'no' into 'yes' through logic. However, you are a *sadhu*. Why are you acting like a lawyer like us?" Srila Sridhar Goswami Maharaja said, "Now it is night. The sun has already set in the western sky. Is it possible to see the sun if we bring all the electric lights of Madras city and shine them towards the sky? Definitely not. But, tomorrow, when the sun rises in the eastern sky, we can naturally see the sun by the sun's own rays. Similarly, through practicing pure devotion, Krishna appears in our heart, spontaneously; then, by the grace of Krishna, we can see Krishna and we can serve Krishna." Thereafter, the lawyer was completely astonished hearing the logical explanation; the lawyer then appreciated Srila Sridhar Goswami Maharaja and the Gaudiya Math.

Srila Sridhar Goswami Maharaja, by nature, was fully free from pride. Therefore, all his godbrothers appreciated his activities. Most of his godbrothers accepted him as their *shiksha guru* (instructing spiritual master). Therefore, we can see that stalwart Gaudiya Math preachers such as Srila Bhakti Prajnan Keshava Goswami Maharaja, Srila Bhakti Saranga Goswami Maharaja, Srila Bhakti Kamal Madhusudan Goswami Maharaja and others took *sannyasa* initiation from him. Also, on several incidents, Srila Bhaktivedanta Swami Goswami Maharaja expressed his gratitude, indicating that he considered Srila Sridhar Goswami Maharaja as his own *shiksha guru*. Srila Sridhar Goswami Maharaja had loving friendly relations with all of his godbrothers.

A few days before Srila Prabhupada's departure, Kunja Babu and Srila Bhakti Rakshak Sridhar Goswami Maharaja were present in Srila Prabhupada's room. Srila Prabhupada instructed Srila Sridhar Goswami Maharaja to sing *Sri Rupa Manjari Pada*. Just as Srila Sridhar Goswami Maharaja was about to sing, Kunja Babu said, "Wait. I will call Pranava. He has a sweet voice." Upon hearing Kunja Babu's call for him, Sripad Pranavananda entered Srila Prabhupada's room and began to sing, as he understood that it was Srila Prabhupada's desire for him to sing. As he sang a few words, Srila Prabhupada interjected and said, "I said that Sridhar Maharaja should sing this song, so let him sing first." Thereafter, Srila Sridhar Goswami Maharaja sang the song *Sri Rupa Manjari Pada*. Immediately after hearing this song, Srila Prabhupada said, "Now, Pranava, sing *Hari He Doyal Mora Jaya Radhanath*." Then, Sripad Pranavananda sang the song. In this manner, Srila Prabhupada respected everyone while simultaneously ensuring that

his instructions were followed. Similarly, Srila Sridhar Goswami Maharaja used to give respect to everyone.

When Srila Prabhupada departed from this world, Srila Bhakti Gaurava Vaikhanas Goswami Maharaja, Srila Bhakti Rakshak Sridhar Goswami Maharaja and Sripad Pranavananda Brahmachari performed Srila Prabhupada's *samadhi* ceremony, according to the request of Kunjabihari Vidyabhushan.

After Srila Prabhupada's physical departure, most of Srila Prabhupada's disciples established various units of the Gaudiya Math in different places. Srila Sridhar Goswami Maharaja established his main preaching unit in the name of Sri Chaitanya Saraswat Math in Koler Danga, Navadwip in the year 1941. Srila Sridhar Goswami Maharaja first moved there alone and lived in a straw hut constantly chanting Hare Krishna *maha-mantra*, worshiping his Giriraj Shila and composing the glorifications of various *acharyas* and the Supreme Lord in Sanskrit poetry. Some of his writings include *Srila Prabhupada Padma-stavakam, Sri Prema-dhama-deva Stotram, Prapanna Jivanamrtam, Nityananda Dasakam, Srimad Bhaktivinoda Viraha Dasakam* and so on. Srila Sridhar Goswami Maharaja's purity in spiritual practice and his pure desire to follow in the footsteps of his *gurudeva*, Srila Prabhupada, magnetically attracted thousands of people to take shelter of his divine lotus feet.

Srila Sridhar Goswami Maharaja's followers collected thousands of hours of his discourses in the English and Bengali languages and published many literatures such as *Sri Guru and His Grace, Guardian of Devotion, The Hidden Treasure of the Sweet Absolute*, etc. Eventually, many branches of Sri Chaitanya Saraswat Math were established throughout India and abroad. However, Srila Sridhar Goswami Maharaja never left India. In his old age, he remained in Mayapur, yet the spiritual vibration

of his potent teachings vibrated throughout the world and inspired many devotees to open branches of Sri Chaitanya Saraswat Math throughout the world.

Srila Bhakti Pramode Puri Goswami Maharaja used to say, "Srila Sridhar Goswami Maharaja is like the Himalaya mountains. The Himalaya mountains don't move anywhere but everyone comes to see the Himalayas. Similarly, Srila Sridhar Goswami Maharaja does not leave Mayapur, but devotees from all over the world come to his lotus feet." He would also say, "Srila Sridhar Goswami Maharaja is filling the gap after the disappearance of Srila Bhaktivinoda Thakura. Srila Sridhar Goswami Maharaja also published many Sanskrit literatures just as Srila Bhaktivinoda Thakura and Srila Rupa Goswamipada did."

A few years before his physical departure, when he was manifesting sickness pastimes, Srila Sridhar Goswami Maharaja appointed his dear disciple Srila Bhakti Sundar Govinda Goswami Maharaja as his successor and allowed him to give initiations in his physical presence. This is a very exceptional action. Through this activity, Srila Sridhar Goswami Maharaja is proving to us that *guru-tattva* is one; Sri Guru is not an individual but is an absolute truth. We should not discriminate that this *guru* is higher than that *guru* and so on. If someone is appointed to be *guru* by his own *guru* who is a pure devotee, then we should accept that pure devotee's appointed successor to be non-different from him.

By the Lord's will, three days before Srila Sridhar Goswami Maharaja's final physical departure. Srila Bhakti Pramode Puri Goswami Maharaja visited him at Sri Chaitanya Saraswat Math, Navadwip. Srila Sridhar Goswami Maharaja requested Srila Bhakti Pramode Puri Goswami Maharaja to stay with him until he would disappear from this world. After three days, Srila

Sridhar Goswami Maharaja physically left this world on 12 August 1988 at Navadwip, Sri Chaitanya Saraswat Math, which is the parent temple of all branches of Sri Chaitanya Saraswat Math. In order to fulfill the will of Srila Sridhar Goswami Maharaja, Srila Bhakti Pramode Puri Goswami Maharaja, who was his dearest godbrother and friend for more than 60 years (since 1923), served as the principal priest of the *samadhi* ceremony. Srila Sridhar Goswami Maharaja's divine body was placed into *samadhi* in the campus of Sri Chaitanya Saraswat Math. Darkness prevailed upon the entire Gaudiya Vaishnava Society after the disappearance of a hidden treasure like Srila Sridhar Goswami Maharaja.

CHAPTER TWENTY-TWO

Srila Bhakti Sambandha Turyashrami Goswami Maharaja

On Tuesday, 26 December 1893 (Bengali Calendar: 12 Poush 1300, Krishna chaturthi – fourth day of the waning-moon cycle), an exalted personality appeared in the home of Janardan Das and Saraswati Devi in the village of Patna, Narail, Jessore, Bangladesh. Seeing the baby boy's beautiful form, his parents named him Bhuvanmohan (he who enchants the entire world).

Bhuvanmohan worked as a manager in a private firm and studied at Khulna, Bangladesh. Srila Prabhupada used to go to Khulna almost every week to preach the divine message of Lord Chaitanya. During one such visit, Bhuvanmohan had the opportunity to see Srila Prabhupada. This darshan alone sparked an eagerness within Bhuvanmohan and, after some time, he went to Bag Bazar Gaudiya Math, Calcutta to personally meet with Srila Prabhupada. After this meeting, he returned home, and his parents tried to arrange his marriage to keep him at home as a householder. He was, however, not interested in getting married; he wanted to lead a renounced life. His attraction to Srila Prabhupada urged him to leave home and take initiation from Srila Prabhupada at Chaitanya Math, Mayapur, Nadia. Srila Prabhupada gave him the name Bhuvaneshwar Das Brahmachari.

After the initiation ceremony, his father came to Chaitanya Math and said, "Bhuvanmohan is the sole breadwinner of the family. All my other sons do not earn any income. Please send Bhuvanmohan back home." Srila Prabhupada replied, "He has come here to do *hari-bhajana*. How can I send him back? It is better if you send your other sons to me so that they can do their studies here." Janardan Das went back home and sent his youngest son, Jamini Das, to Srila Prabhupada. Srila

Prabhupada helped Jamini study until the completion of his Master of Arts (M.A.) degree.

Gradually, Bhuvaneshwar Brahmachari studied all devotional scriptures with sincerity and followed in the footsteps of Srila Prabhupada with love from the bottom of his heart. On Friday, 2 March 1934 (Bengali calendar: 18 Phalgun 1340, Gaura Purnima) Srila Prabhupada gave Bhuvaneshwar Das Brahmachari *sannyasa* at Srila Gaura Kishore Das Babaji Maharaja's *samadhi* temple located at Chaitanya Math, Mayapur. His new name became Bhakti Sambandha Turyashrami Goswami Maharaja.

Turyashrami Goswami Maharaja wrote many poems and articles. Srila Prabhupada appointed him to become temple president of the Gaudiya Math branch in Delhi, a service which he performed devoutly. Three years later, Srila Prabhupada physically passed away from this world. Hearing this distressful news, Turyashrami Goswami Maharaja went to Chaitanya Math to see Srila Prabhupada's *samadhi*. Out of separation, Turyashrami Goswami Maharaja decided to perform solitary devotional practice. Turyashrami Goswami Maharaja went to Bordia, Jessore, Bangladesh and, with the help of the local devotees, established a temple, Sri Sri Gaura Saraswat Gaudiya Math. He installed the deities of Sri Sri Guru Gauranga Gandharvika Giridhari. Due to Maharaja's attractive personality, many people were drawn to take shelter of him.

On 22 November 1978 (Bengali calendar: 6 Agrahayana 1385, Krishna Saptami, the seventh day of the waning-moon cycle) during the early hours of the morning (*brahma-muhurta*), Srila Turyashrami Goswami Maharaja left this material world while chanting the holy name and went back to the spiritual abode to join the eternal service of the Divine Couple, Sri Sri Radha-Krishna.

CHAPTER TWENTY-THREE

SRILA BHAKTI SARANGA GOSWAMI MAHARAJA

One of those significant personalities who appeared to assist Srila Prabhupada in his mission appeared on 3 February 1888 (Bengali calendar: Vaishakh Krishna Sasthi 1294) in the village of Patrasaya, Bankura District, West Bengal. He was born in a high-class *brahmana* Bandopadhyay family. His father, Ramachandra Bandopadhyay, and his mother, Srimati Jnanada Sundari Devi, were both spiritually inclined. They named their newborn son Atul Chandra Bandopadhyay. His parents worshiped their family deities, Sri Sri Radha-Shyamsundar, on a daily basis in their home. Since childhood, Atul Chandra was attentive towards his parents' ritualistic practice of worship.

According to Bengali tradition, at six months, before feeding a child his first grains, a test is done to determine the child's future inclination. A plate is arranged with various items (i.e., coins, gold, *durva* grass, *Srimad Bhagavad Gita*, dry mud and a colorful fragrant flower) and placed in front of the child. The item that the child reaches for first is an indication of the child's inherent nature. When this plate was put in front of Atul Chandra, the baby grabbed the *Srimad Bhagavad Gita*. After the incident, many scholarly persons expressed their opinions that this baby would be a great saint in the near future.

Atul Chandra was a meritorious student in his reputed village school. In his youth, he paid obeisance to his parents and to his grandmother every day. By their blessings, Atul Chandra realized the essence of *Srimad Bhagavad Gita, Srimad Bhagavatam* as well as the other authenticated scriptures. Since childhood, he was generous in helping the poor and destitute.

When Atul Chandra was in college, he arranged a religious debate amongst students. In that debate, some glorified *jnana*, some glorified *karma* and some glorified austerity and yoga. According to the Lord's arrangement,

Atul Chandra was the last speaker; he defeated everybody's logic and established *bhakti* as the supreme path to attain the Supreme Lord and to deliver oneself from the miserable material condition that plagues us.

In the year 1910, an international conference was arranged in his college to discuss various philosophies. Therein, Atul Chandra gave a magnificent lecture in English about devotional philosophy. In the audience, amongst others, there was a railway commissioner who was extremely happy hearing his talk. After receiving his degree in 1910, Atul Chandra was appointed by the railway department as an engineer in Dhanbad, Jharkhand. Coincidently, the railway superintendent was a person named Atul Chandra Datta.

While serving in Dhanbad, Atul Chandra Bandopadhyay met with a disciple of Srila Prabhupada named Professor Nishikanta Sanyal. Atul Chandra Bandopadhyay, Atul Chandra Datta and Prof. Nishikanta Sanyal had daily discussions about spirituality. During these discussions, Prof. Nishikanta Sanyal frequently spoke of the glories of Srila Prabhupada.

Once, Atul Chandra Datta and Atul Chandra Bandopadhyay decided to visit Sri Chaitanya Math in Mayapur to meet with Srila Prabhupada. It was a hot summer's day, and they reached Sri Chaitanya Math at about 14:00. Vinode Da (later known as Srila Bhakti Prajnan Keshava Goswami Maharaja) greeted both of them, asked them to freshen up and then arranged for them to honor *prasadam*. After lunch, Vinode Da took them to meet Srila Prabhupada in his *bhajan kutir*. Both of them were completely mesmerized seeing Srila Prabhupada's holy form and decided to stay a few days to listen to Srila Prabhupada's ecstatic descriptions of *bhakti*. Day by day, Atul Chandra Bandopadhyay was becoming more and more inclined towards renunciation.

His mother, out of fear, arranged his marriage. Although he got married, his mood was like Raghunath Das Goswami's; inclined towards renunciation and devoting his life to spirituality and Srila Prabhupada's mission. At that time, upon request from Prof. Nishikanta Sanyal and Atul Chandra Datta, Srila Prabhupada came to Dhanbad. They hosted Srila Prabhupada in the railway quarters of Atul Chandra Bandopadhyay. There, Srila Prabhupada gave attractive discourses on the benefit of chanting the holy name (Hare Krishna *maha-mantra*) in the *Kali-yuga*. During this trip, several railway officers, along with Atul Chandra Bandopadhyay, took initiation from Srila Prabhupada. Srila Prabhupada gave Atul Chandra Bandopadhyay the name Sri Aprakrita Bhakti Saranga Prabhu. After initiation, whenever he was on leave from his work, Bhakti Saranga Prabhu spent as much time as possible with Srila Prabhupada. Also, when his office hours were completed, he would go and collect alms from various reputed households for the service of Sri Chaitanya Math, his *gurudeva's* mission.

Once, in 1919, Srila Bhakti Vivek Bharati Goswami Maharaja and Srila Bhakti Swarupa Parvat Goswami Maharaja went to Dhanbad to collect donations for the construction of devotee quarters at Sri Chaitanya Math, Mayapur. Bhakti Saranga Prabhu hosted them and, after hearing the desire of Srila Prabhupada from them, felt blessed for the service opportunity. He took them to a coalmine manager who, upon hearing the request of Bhakti Saranga Prabhu, gave five wagons full of coal. The coal would be used in the preparation of the bricks used to construct the devotee quarters.

At the age of 32, Bhakti Saranga Prabhu resigned from his work and came to the lotus feet of his *gurudeva* at Ultadingi Junction Road, Calcutta with his entire provident fund. Seeing his service attitude and spiritual

scholarship, Srila Prabhupada gave him the titles 'Bhakti Shastri Maha-mahopadeshak' (highly qualified spiritual instructor) and 'Praudha Sevadhikari' (experienced servitor). Srila Prabhupada appointed him to become the main editor of the weekly *Gaudiya* magazine. On 15 August 1925, Srila Prabhupada established an editorial board for all *Gaudiya* publications called the Gaudiya Sampadak Mandali and appointed Bhakti Saranga Prabhu as the chairman. For 16 years from 1920 to 1936, Bhakti Saranga Prabhu served as the chief editor of the weekly *Gaudiya* magazine.

Once, Srila Prabhupada was unhappy because a scholar criticized Srila Bhaktivinoda Thakura. Srila Prabhupada sent Bhakti Saranga Prabhu to that scholar, and he completely defeated the criticisms of the scholar. The scholar accepted his defeat and surrendered to Srila Prabhupada. Another time, Bhakti Saranga Prabhu was physically unwell, but it was the day of a *nagar sankirtan* program. Srila Prabhupada asked him, "Are you physically well?" Immediately, to satisfy Srila Prabhupada, Bhakti Saranga Prabhu said, "Yes". Srila Prabhupada said, "If we always engage our minds in serving the Divine Couple, the mind will always be healthy. If the mind is healthy, then the body will be healthy. Through service of the Divine Couple, we are eligible to become free from material attachment. In this way, having gotten this rare human birth, one gains spiritual power through serving Sri Guru and Vaishnava. Through that power, all obstacles will pass away."

On 1 November 1936, Bhakti Saranga Prabhu boarded a ship, the Phoenix, from Colombo, Sri Lanka to London. On 4 November 1936 on the way to London, he had a vision of Srila Prabhupada in the sky; Srila Prabhupada said, "Your preaching in the West will be extremely successful. The mercy of *guru* is

everything." On 18 November, he reached London. Samvidananda Prabhu, who was a barrister by profession and a disciple of Srila Prabhupada and the brother of Srila Bhakti Vilas Tirtha Goswami Maharaja, brought him to the Gaudiya Math at 3 Glosterhouse, London. In London, Bhakti Saranga Prabhu gave spiritual discourses in various prominent assemblies. He was very successful.

However, during this time, Srila Prabhupada physically passed away. Bhakti Saranga Prabhu returned to India on 23 September 1937. Upon his return, out of intense separation from Srila Prabhupada, Bhakti Saranga Prabhu decided to go back to his village to reside in a solitary place. Seeing his condition, all his godbrothers requested him to take *sannyasa* initiation. On 20 March 1941 (Bengali calendar: 6 Chaitra 1347) at Tota Gopinath Temple in the presence of Srila Bhakti Vichar Jajabar Goswami Maharaja, Srila Bhakti Gaurav Vaikhanas Goswami Maharaja and Srila Bhakti Prakash Aranya Goswami Maharaja, he took the vows of *sannyasa* from Srila Bhakti Rakshak Sridhar Goswami Maharaja and received the name Srila Bhakti Saranga Goswami Maharaja. Afterwards, Srila Bhakti Saranga Goswami Maharaja established a temple at Imli-tala in Vrindavan, the place where Chaitanya Mahaprabhu sat when He had visited Vrindavan. He also established temples at Karol Bag, Delhi, at Balur Ghat, Calcutta, and so on. In Sridham Mayapur, he established a Sri Sri Gaur Nityananda temple at the place where Sri Chaitanya Mahaprabhu and Sri Nityananda Prabhu met for the first time.

On Tuesday, 26 May 1964 (Bengali Calendar 12 Jyeshta 1371) at his temple in Calcutta, Srila Bhakti Saranga Goswami Maharaja entered into the eternal pastimes of Sri Sri Radha-Govinda leaving this material world behind. His *samadhi* was established in the presence of his godbrothers at his Mayapur temple.

CHAPTER TWENTY-FOUR

Srila
Bhakti Sarvasva
Giri Goswami
Maharaja

In the year 1890 (Bengali calendar year 1306), a ray of Srila Prabhupada was born in Dhaka in an aristocratic family. This boy, named Indubabu, was renounced from childhood, showing indifference towards food, distaste in games and grave disposition. He preferred associating with saintly persons and took much interest in religion and spirituality. His parents were worried, thinking the boy was cursed by some higher entity or that he had some bad planetary influence. They would anxiously pray to the Supreme Lord for their child to have an auspicious life.

In Kartik month, November 1912 (Bengali calendar year 1328), Srila Prabhupada, Srila Bhakti Pradipa Tirtha Goswami Maharaja and various saints came to a wealthy landowner's home in Dhaka and gave discourses on the *Srimad Bhagavatam*, which were attended by Indubabu. Shortly thereafter, Indubabu received initiation from Srila Prabhupada and was given the new name Sri Gaurendu Brahmachari.

In 1922 (Bengali calendar year 1328), Sri Gaurendu Brahmachari published the fourth edition of Srila Bhaktivinoda Thakura's book *Saranagati* from Sri Madhva Gaudiya Math, Dhaka. In 1924, he preached with his godbrother Srila Bhakti Vijnana Ashram Goswami Maharaja in Ganjam, Odisha. In 1925, during Navadwip Mandal Parikrama, Sri Gaurendu was instructed by Srila Prabhupada to give a discourse on the pastimes of Lord Hari in the English language at Antpur station near Sri Paramesvari Thakura's *sripat*. His discourse was appreciated by all.

In 1925 (Bengali calendar 29 Bhadra 1332), he received *sannyasa* (renounced order) from Srila Prabhupada with the name Srila Bhakti Sarvasva Giri Goswami Maharaja. He was a fearless orator and preached all over India under Srila Prabhupada's instruction. He met with the British government's viceroy and was greatly appreciated along with a certificate. Srila Prabhupada was very happy and mentioned how pleased he was with Srila Giri Goswami Maharaja's spreading the message of Lord Chaitanya all over India. Many government officers, governors and viceroys glorified Srila Giri Goswami Maharaja's preaching efforts and expressed enthusiasm in the spreading of Lord Chaitanya's philosophy of non-sectarian and non-judgmental divine love. Srila Giri Goswami Maharaja's style of speaking and writing in English was unique and was glorified by scholars such as Raven's College Professor of History and Sri Nishikanta Sanyal (Sri Padmanarayan Das Bhakti Sudhakara Prabhu) from Cuttack, Odisha.

Srila Giri Goswami Maharaja was of pure character, had a childlike simplicity, was pleased with whatever he had, was strongly fixed in service to his spiritual master and glorified the Supreme Lord everywhere. He served in various ways at Srila Prabhupada's established centers in Mayapur, Calcutta, Dhaka, Patna, Allahabad, Kurukshetra and so on, looking after preaching Mahaprabhu's teachings in the form of discourses, books, and weekly magazines. He also engaged in various services related to Mayapur, Vrindavan and Puri. Srila Giri Goswami Maharaja was instrumental in establishing the Gaudiya Math center in Rangoon, Myanmar, as well as the Gaudiya Maths in Lucknow and Haridwar.

After Srila Prabhupada's physical departure in 1937, Srila Giri Goswami Maharaja began to also serve as a member of the managing board of Srila Bhakti Dayita Madhava Goswami Maharaja's Sri Gaudiya Sanskrit Vidyalaya located in Ishodyan, Mayapur. He further fulfilled the role of chairman of the yearly Gaura Purnima Chaitanya Vani Pracharini Sabha and gave discourses. He would also attend the biannual preaching

programs of Sri Chaitanya Gaudiya Math located in
South Calcutta.

Srila Giri Goswami Maharaja gave the Kaliya Daha
Mandir which he had established to Srila Bhakti Dayita
Madhava Goswami Maharaja towards the end of his
life. Srila Madhava Goswami Maharaja always took care
of Srila Giri Goswami Maharaja's health expenses and
needs by sending various people from his Vrindavan
branch of Sri Chaitanya Gaudiya Math to take care of
Srila Giri Goswami Maharaja whenever it was required.
On Friday, 3 November 1967 (16 Kartik) at the age of 68,
Srila Giri Goswami Maharaja departed from this world
in Vrindavan at 20:05, after having completed the Giriraj
Govardhan *puja* and Annakut Mahotsav earlier that day.
At the last moments of his physical presence, Srila Giri
Goswami Maharaja cried out, "Prabhupada, protect me!
Have mercy on me. Forgive me for all my offenses. Give
me a place at your lotus feet." His godbrothers, including
Srila Bhakti Hridaya Bon Goswami Maharaja (who had

taken *sannyasa* on the same day as Srila Giri Goswami Maharaja), Srila Bhaktyaloka Paramahamsa Goswami Maharaja, Srila Bhakti Saurabh Bhaktisar Goswami Maharaja, Srila Bhakti Subrata Paramarthi Goswami Maharaja and many other devotees, had come to see him just before his passing. According to Srila Bon Goswami Maharaja's instructions, Srila Giri Goswami Maharaja was placed in *samadhi* at Sri Vinoda-vani Gaudiya Math near Srila Sanatan Goswami's *samadhi* at Sri Sri Radha-Madanmohan's temple.

CHAPTER TWENTY-FIVE

SRILA
BHAKTI SARVASVA
SATYA GOVINDA
GOSWAMI MAHARAJA

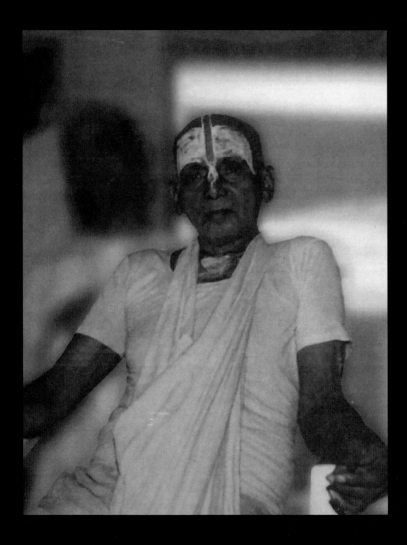

S rila Bhakti Sarvasva Satya Govinda Goswami Maharaja was born in the year 1914 (428 Gaurabda) in order to bestow auspiciousness upon the residents of the material world. He was named Santosh and was the youngest of five sons born to Sri Taraka Candra and Srimati Padmavati Devi, who lived in Laksminathpur, Uttar 24 Parganas, West Bengal.

After finishing his material education in the year 1932, he was attracted by the preaching of four pure devotees, namely, His Divine Grace Bhakti Vivek Bharati Goswami Maharaja, His Divine Grace Bhakti Srirupa Siddhanti Goswami Maharaja, His Divine Grace Bhakti Dayita Madhava Goswami Maharaja and Navin Krishna Vidyalankar Prabhu. On an auspicious day in the month of Ashwin, Sri Santosh received *harinama* (first initiation) from Srila Prabhupada at Bag Bazar Sri Gaudiya Math. At this time, by the mercy of Srila Prabhupada, Sri Santosh Kumar received the name Sriman Satya Govinda Das Brahmachari.

On Phalguna Purnima of the same year, on the appearance day of Sriman Mahaprabhu, Srila Prabhupada saw Sriman Satya Govinda Das Brahmachari's eagerness and gave him *diksha* (second initiation). After initiation, in accordance with Srila Prabhupada's instructions, Sriman Satya Govinda Das Brahmachari assisted with the publications of the *math* under the guidance of Pranavananda Brahmachari Mahopadeshak Pratnavidyalankar (later known as Srila Bhakti Pramode Puri Goswami Maharaja). For a long time, he also served at Sri Chaitanya Math under the guidance of Srimad Bhakti Vilas Tirtha Goswami Maharaja, sharing loving relations with his godbrothers.

In the year 1992, in accordance with the instruction he received in a dream from Sri Varshabhanavi Radha Thakurani, Sriman Satya Govinda Das Brahmachari

accepted *sannyasa* (the fourth order) from his godbrother Srila Bhakti Pramode Puri Goswami Maharaja. In order to keep remembrance of the name given by Srila Prabhupada, he was given the name Srimad Bhakti Sarvasva Satya Govinda Maharaja. He was a perfected instrument in the service of his spiritual master. In 1999, Srila Maharaja left the material world while staying at Purushottam Gaudiya Math, a branch of Sri Chaitanya Math situated near *bhajan kutir* and the *samadhi* temple of Nama-Acharya Haridas Thakura. His body was cremated at Swarga Dwar, Puri, Odisha.

SRILA BHAKTI SAUDHA ASHRAM GOSWAMI MAHARAJA

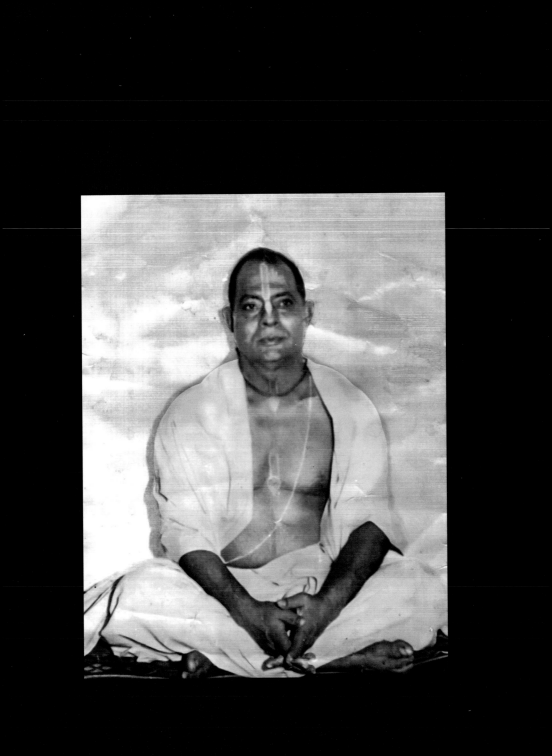

One of Srila Prabhupada's rays appeared in a village of Faridpur district, Bangladesh in a landlord family on 28 April 1914 on Akshay Tritiya, the starting day of Lord Jagannath's Chandan Yatra (Bengali calendar: third day of the waxing moon, Vaisakh Shukla Trtiya). He was named Bhupendranath Chattopadhyay. His father was Yogendranath Chattopadhyay, and his mother was Vilasini Devi. When Bhupendranath was three years old, his parents suddenly passed away within ten days of each other. Thereafter, Bhupendranath came to his maternal grandfather's house at Raadikhaal, Dhaka district, Bangladesh. Under the guidance of his maternal grandfather, Bhupendranath got his Bachelor of Science degree from Bongabasi College, Calcutta.

By nature, Bhupendranath was soft, generous and helpful to others in every aspect. Once, he got one of Srila Prabhupada's books and read Srila Prabhupada's instruction "We have not come here in this temporary life to become great workers, scholars, religionists or donators. The nondual Absolute Truth is Sri Vrajendranandana, who came in the most merciful form of Bhagavan Sri Krishna Chaitanya Mahaprabhu. The supreme and topmost goal of life can only be gained through the execution of pure and beautiful devotional service to Sri Krishna Chaitanya Mahaprabhu. Coming into this material world in the human form of life is meant for engaging in spiritual practice. This is our utmost duty. There is nothing more to be said." After reading this instruction, Bhupendranath's heart was transformed.

With the help of two of Srila Prabhupada's disciples, namely Bhakti Kankan Tapasvi Goswami Maharaja and Sriman Navadwip Prabhu, Bhupendranath got the chance to meet Srila Prabhupada face to face. On 8 May 1935, Bhupendranath received *harinama* and *diksha* (first and second initiation) from Srila Prabhupada at Bag Bazar Gaudiya Math and received the name Bhutabhrt Das Brahmachari. After initiation, Bhutabhrt Prabhu served Srila Prabhupada's loving mission under the guidance of Navadwip Das Prabhu. Bhutabhrt Brahmachari was able to speak English well, along with 10 other languages. Srila Prabhupada engaged him as a teacher at the Bhaktivinoda Institute in Mayapur. In 1936, Srila Prabhupada sent Bhutabhrt Brahmachari to Chennai (previously known as Madras) as the temple in-charge. Bhutabhrt Prabhu's execution of his services such as preaching activities, temple management, etc., pleased Srila Prabhupada. Bhutabhrt Prabhu used to preach with Hayagriva Das Brahmachari (later known as Bhakti Dayita Madhava Goswami Maharaja) in Assam.

In 1937, as soon as Bhutabhrt Prabhu heard the news of Srila Prabhupada's physical departure, he fainted out of intense separation. At that time, Srila Prabhupada appeared in his dream and said, "Don't cry. I will accept all your service. Please go ahead with your service of spreading the message of Rupa Goswami, Sanatana Goswami, Raghunath Das Goswami and Bhaktivinoda Thakura with full enthusiasm." In order to fulfill Srila Prabhupada's instruction, in 1939, Bhutabhrt Prabhu went to Rangoon, Myanmar to preach. Due to intense separation from Srila Prabhupada, Bhutabhrt Prabhu felt that he should perform solitary bhajan and decided to reside in a school located in Bhawanipur, Calcutta.

Eventually, in 1952, he took the renounced order (*sannyasa*) from Bhakti Gaurav Vaikhanas Goswami Maharaja at Tota Gopinath temple, Jagannath Puri Dham and received the name Bhakti Saudha Ashram Goswami Maharaja. Srila Ashram Goswami Maharaja visited many pilgrimage places and performed his spiritual practice. He opened two preaching centers, called Bhakti

Saudha Bhajan Kutir in Mayapur and Sri Chaitanya Math in Dumdum, Calcutta. In February 1982, during his stay at the Calcutta center, Srila Ashram Goswami Maharaja began to manifest sickness pastimes. On the night of 31 March 1982, he had the desire to get a full body check-up at a medical center for further treatment, but it was the Lord's desire to take him on that same night. According to the English calendar, at 02:30 on 1 April 1982, all the devotees who were at the Calcutta center heard the words "Hare Krishna" coming from his room in a loud voice. When they entered the room, they all saw that Srila Ashram Goswami Maharaja had physically passed away and had entered into the eternal pastimes of Sri Sri Radha-Govinda. His physical form was taken to Bhakti Saudha Bhajan Kutir in Mayapur, where they established the *samadhi*. A *pushpa samadhi* was established at Sri Sri Radha-Damodar *mandir* in Vrindavan.

CHAPTER TWENTY-SEVEN

SRILA BHAKTI SAURABH BHAKTISAR GOSWAMI MAHARAJA

Our previous teachers have taught us that just a glimpse of a pure devotee of the Lord is the greatest fortune of all. A moment of such association can immediately purify our *chitta* (our mind, our heart, our consciousness, our intelligence) and instantly bring one to the stage of perfection. Such potency was observed in the personality of Srila Prabhupada. A moment of association with the books of Srila Prabhupada had such a transformative purifying effect on the life of Sri Nanda Gopal. Although he had not met with Srila Prabhupada, he was captured by the logical delivery of devotional service from His Divine Grace in his books and was inspired with the desire to meet the author.

Sri Nanda Gopal was born in a reputed *brahmana* (Bandapadhaya) family in 1902 in the village of Chandani Mohal, Khulna district, Bangladesh. His parents' names were Sri Shashadhar Bandopadhyaya and Srimati Shailabala Devi.

Since childhood Nanda Gopal was a good student at school. In his matriculation examination, Sri Nanda Gopal passed with impressive results. To further his studies, he gained admission to Cuttack Engineering college in Odisha. While studying at college, he would often visit the Sri Gaudiya Math in Cuttack. There, he met with Srila Brajabihari Das Babaji Maharaja and by his grace, he got the opportunity to study many spiritual books published by Srila Prabhupada. Although Sri Nanda Gopal had not yet met with Srila Prabhupada, he was enamored by the logical

conclusions of his books, which inspired him to meet him.

Even though his father noticed that his son had become more interested in the study of the scriptures by the Gaudiya Math than in his academic engineering studies, he did not oppose his son's interest. Shashadhar Bandapadhaya was more concerned about his son's deliverance from this mundane existence and to Sri Chaitanya Math in Mayapur. *Srimad Bhagavatam* states that one is considered a real father if he is able to deliver his children from the impending cycle of birth and death. Having his son's spiritual interest in mind, he was considered the best of fathers. A few days before Lord Chaitanya's appearance ceremony, Gaura Purnima, Sri Nanda Gopal and his parents arrived in Mayapur to attend the festival. There, they met with Srila Prabhupada and felt instant attraction to him. On the day of Gaura Purnima, Srila Prabhupada gave them first and second initiation. After initiation, Sri Nanda Gopal was known as Nanda Dulal Das Brahmachari. Thereafter, he remained in the *math* under the shelter of his beloved spiritual master, giving up all attachment to family life.

His mood of service was very attractive and pleased all the temple devotees. As a result, they favorably reported the good character of Nanda Dulal to Srila Prabhupada. By the grace of Srila Prabhupada, Nanda Dulal Prabhu received the title of 'Bhaktitul', which means 'devotionally inspiring'. Shortly afterwards, Nanda Dulal Brahmachari was engaged by Srila Prabhupada as a teacher in Sri Bhaktivinoda institute, where he served as a teacher for a long time. After Srila Prabhupada's physical departure, most of the godbrothers established different *maths* of Lord Chaitanya's preaching mission.

Sripad Nanda Dulal Brahmachari decided to take *sannyasa* initiation from his favorite godbrother, Srila

Bhakti Saranga Goswami Maharaja. He was given the name Srila Bhakti Saurabh Bhaktisar Goswami Maharaja (Bhaktisar Goswami Maharaja). Eventually, he established a few *maths* of Lord Sri Chaitanya's preaching mission in the name of Sri Gauranga Gaudiya Math, at Mayapur; Sri Nityananda Gaudiya Math at Birbhum; Sri Radha Govinda Gaudiya Math, Kendran, Burdwan; Sri Bhaktisar Gaudiya Math, at Vrindavan, Sri Narasimha Gaudiya Math, at Puri, Odisha.

Srila Bhaktisar Goswami Maharaja's nature was to stay away from all material adoration, name, fame and recognition. In his old age he was fully absorbed in chanting the Holy Name (Hare Krishna *maha-mantra*). During that period, to whoever came to hear *harikatha* (discourses) from him, he would say, "I have spoken much, and you all have heard much from me. If you follow me, then I am sure that all of you will progress in your spiritual practice properly and gradually reach your final destination, the abode of Sri Sri Radha-Krishna, Goloka Vrindavan."

On 14 July 1995 at 05:10 at Sri Gauranga Gaudiya Math, Mayapur Srila Bhaktisar Goswami Maharaja physically left this world in the presence of his favorite disciples, such as Bhakti Lalit Madhava Maharaja, Bhakti Sundar Sadhu Maharaja, Bhakti Sudhir Acharya Maharaja, etc. Presently Srila Bhakti Sudhir Acharya Maharaja is continuing his mission as his successor.

CHAPTER TWENTY-EIGHT

SRILA BHAKTI SRIRUPA BHAGAVAT GOSWAMI MAHARAJA

Amongst the rays ('manpower') sent to Srila Prabhupada by Lord Sri Chaitanya Mahaprabhu was Srila Bhakti Srirupa Bhagavat Goswami Maharaja. He was born in 1906, during full moon, on the special bathing ceremony (Snana Yatra) day of Lord Jagannath, in the village of Rudaghara, Khulna district, Bangladesh. His father, Sri Sitanath Haldar, and mother, Srimati Kumudini Devi, were both extremely happy to see the effulgent baby boy. He was named Rupalal, which means a boy of beautiful red color.

From childhood, Sri Rupalal made efforts to keep appropriate equilibrium between his academic and spiritual practices. He had a daily routine of reading *Srimad Bhagavad Gita*. Upon completion of his academic studies, he decided to spend some time in a holy place. He came to Gaya, a significant holy place for those of the Hindu and Buddhist faiths. In March 1935, while Rupalal was in Gaya visiting his relatives, Srila Prabhupada also visited Gaya with his preaching team. There, Srila Prabhupada's logical discourses on the *Srimad Bhagavatam* inspired Rupalal to lead a renounced life. In November of the same year, Srila Prabhupada came to Gaya temple again for a deity installation ceremony. This time, through Srila Prabhupada's causeless mercy, Rupalal received *harinama* and *diksha* (first and second initiation) from Srila Prabhupada, as well as the name Rupavilas Das Brahmachari (Rupavilas Prabhu). Seeing Rupavilas Prabhu's sincerity of spiritual practice and compelling temple management ability, in a short space of time Srila Prabhupada appointed him as Gaya's temple president.

After Srila Prabhupada physical departure, all *Gaudiya* devotees were immersed in pangs of separation and were feeling a lack of spiritual inspiration. While almost everyone was in this state, Sri Rupavilas Prabhu continued to perform Srila Prabhupada's services under

the supervision of Srila Puri Das Thakura, who was previously known as Sripad Ananta Vasudeva Prabhu. Eventually, his talents and service mood made him editor of the *Bhagavat* magazine in both the Bengali and Hindi languages. In 1938, Sripad Rupavilas Prabhu's spiritual realization and various skillful devotional publications allowed him to get the spiritual title 'Vidyarnav', which means ocean of knowledge, from Srila Puri Das Thakura.

For a span of 28 years, from September 1954 to 1982, Sri Rupavilas Prabhu continued his most important service as General Secretary of Sri Gaudiya Mission. During that period, Srila Bhakti Kevala Audolumi Goswami Maharaja was the presiding *acharya* of Gaudiya

Mission. In 1969, seeing Sri Rupavilas Prabhu's sincere effort to look after all missionary services, Srila Audolumi Maharaja happily gave him *sannyasa*. Sri Rupavilas Prabhu received the name Srila Bhakti Srirupa Bhagavat Goswami Maharaja.

After Srila Audolumi Goswami Maharaja's physical departure, Srila Bhagavat Goswami Maharaja was unanimously elected to become *acharya* of Gaudiya Mission in 1982. Whilst in the *acharya* post, Srila Bhagavat Goswami Maharaja opened a new temple of the Gaudiya Mission at Mughalsarai, Uttar Pradesh.

In 1987, in order to bestow his mercy upon the conditioned souls, Srila Bhagavat Goswami Maharaja went to London (UK) along with his intimate associates, namely Sripad Nyasi Maharaja, Sripad Nandadulal Prabhu and Sripad Ananta Madhava Prabhu. In 1992, Srila Bhagavat Goswami Maharaja intellectually and gloriously renovated the old temple of the Mumbai Gaudiya Math which was established by Srila Prabhupada.

The ultimate truth for all living beings is that they must leave their mortal bodies. Srila Bhagavat Goswami Maharaja left his body on 12 February 1993 at the Mumbai temple. However, his exemplary devotional teachings are keeping him alive eternally in the hearts of all *Gaudiya* devotees. Srila Bhagavat Goswami Maharaja's tongue was constantly dancing, chanting the Hare Krishna *maha-mantra* or giving *harikatha*. He was an example of *kīrtanīyaḥ sadā hariḥ*, which means eternally chanting the glories of Lord Hari, in the lineage of Srila Prabhupada.

According to the desire of Srila Bhagavat Goswami Maharaja, his visible transcendental body was buried in the premises of Sri Bhaktisiddhanta Saraswati Thakura Gaudiya Math, Godrumdwip, Swarupgunj, Nadia, West Bengal.

CHAPTER TWENTY-NINE

SRILA
BHAKTI SRIRUPA
SIDDHANTI GOSWAMI
MAHARAJA

This ray of Srila Prabhupada appeared in present-day Bangladesh in Sachilapur, Borishal District, on 12 October 1906 (Bengali calendar: Kartik Shukla Panchami 1303, 5th day of the waxing-moon cycle), in a pious wealthy family and was named Shivashankar. His father was Gopal Chandra De and his mother, Srimati Rajalakshmi Devi. From childhood, Shivashankar was of good character, truthful, talented and helpful to others. Since his childhood, he was studious and generous. He was inclined towards serving holy, renounced persons (*sadhus* and *sannyasis*).

Once, when Shivashankar was 17 years old, he heard that a renounced person from the Gaudiya Math was coming to their area. Shivashankar and his friend went to attend the devotional program and heard from the *sannyasi's* discourse that the Supreme Lord is one without a second. That *sannyasi* was Srila Bhakti Vivek Bharati Goswami Maharaja. After hearing Srila Bharati Goswami Maharaja's discourse, Shivashankar decided to take shelter of Srila Bharati Goswami Maharaja. However, Srila Bharati Goswami Maharaja took Shivashankar to Mayapur and brought him to the shelter of his *gurudeva*, Srila Prabhupada.

In 1924, on the holy day of Lord Chaitanya Mahaprabhu's appearance (Gaura Purnima*)*, Shivashankar received *harinama* and *diksha* (first and second initiation) from Srila Prabhupada and was named Siddhasvarupa Das Brahmachari. Siddhasvarupa Prabhu went back to complete his studies, and in 1928, returned to Srila Prabhupada to join as a full time renounced *brahmachari* and assisted Srila Bhakti Pradip Tirtha Goswami Maharaja, Srila Bhakti Vivek Bharati Goswami Maharaja and Srila Bhakti Rakshak Sridhar Dev Goswami Maharaja in the preaching efforts across Bengal, Bihar, Odisha, Tamil Nadu and Andhra Pradesh.

Once, in present-day Kishoreganj, Mymensingh District, Bangladesh, Siddhasvarupa Das Brahmachari spoke in an assembly of spiritual debate (*sanatana-dharma sabha*) on the topic of *yata mat tata path* – "There are many paths to achieve the same goal." Through proper logic, Siddhasvarupa Prabhu attempted to defeat this concept of *yata mat tata path*. However, the whole audience blindly protested against Siddhasvarupa Prabhu's presentation and stopped him without a proper logical reason. The next day, all major newspapers, such as the *Ananda Bazar Newspaper*, covered the incident and featured an article on the Gaudiya Math. Srila Prabhupada happily spoke in relation to this incident: "Siddhasvarupa's remarks and the subsequent effects have manifested the fruits of ten years of preaching in just one day." Siddhasvarupa Brahmachari used to speak the message of truth without any hesitation. Thus, he spread Srila Prabhupada's logical explanations of the scriptures all over India.

In 1937, after Srila Prabhupada's physical departure, all the disciples were feeling the pangs of separation. To propagate Lord Chaitanya Mahaprabhu's loving mission, Srila Bhakti Vivek Bharati Goswami Maharaja and Siddhasvarupa Prabhu opened a new center in the name of Sri Sarasvata Gaudiya Asana and Mission. In 1941, on the day of Vijaya Dasami, commemorating the day Lord Ramachandra conquered over Ravana's kingdom at Lanka, Siddhasvarupa Prabhu took the renounced order (*sannyasa*) from his senior godbrother Srila Bhakti Prasun Bodhayan Goswami Maharaja and received the name Srila Bhakti Srirupa Siddhanti Goswami Maharaja.

He later established a center at 29 B Hazra Road, Calcutta. After Srila Bharati Goswami Maharaja's physical departure in 1947, Srila Siddhanti Goswami Maharaja felt much separation but continued the preaching mission and established centers in Jagannath

Puri and Navadwip Dham. Srila Siddhanti Goswami Maharaja published Srila Baladeva Vidyabhushan's *Govinda-Bhashya* commentary, Srila Baladeva Vidyabhushan's *Bhagavad Gita* commentary, the *Vedanta-sutras,* as well as many rare *Upanishads.* He would often say, "He who glorifies Lord Hari is in actuality a generous person."

On Friday 4 October 1985 (Bengali calendar: 18 *Ashwin Krishna-Sasthi* 1392, sixth day of the waning moon) at 1:05 am, Srila Siddhanti Goswami Maharaja physically departed at the Calcutta temple located on Hazra Road. His desire was to be cremated, and his disciples established a *pushpa-samadhi* with his ashes at the Jagannath Puri temple and the Navadwip temple situated at Radha Bazar. According to Srila Siddhanti Goswami Maharaja's will, the present temple president and *acharya* is Srila Bhakti Ranjan Sagar Goswami Maharaja (disciple of Srila Siddhanti Goswami Maharaja), who is continuing the mission.

CHAPTER THIRTY

SRILA BHAKTI SWARUPA PARVAT GOSWAMI MAHARAJA

Lord Chaitanya's spiritual descendants and pure devotees are born in different places in the world, but Lord Chaitanya pulls all of them together to His lotus feet at Mayapur. Srila Bhakti Swarupa Parvat Goswami Maharaja was so dear to Lord Chaitanya. By the grace of his *gurudeva*, Srila Prabhupada, and by Lord Chaitanya's desire, Srila Parvat Maharaja was born in Godrumadvipa in 1884 on the day of Guru Purnima. He was named Badol. We know that Godrumadvipa is representative of congregational chanting (*sankirtanakhya-dvipa*). His father was Panchu Gopal Vedanta Desika and, his mother was a disciple of Bhaktivinoda Thakura.

During his childhood, he would often listen to *harikatha* from Srila Bhaktivinoda Thakura at Svananda-sukhada-kunja. Bhaktivinoda Thakura's holy discourses were so attractive that this little boy, Badol, would go to Svananda-sukhada-kunja at midnight in order to listen to the holy pastimes of Lord Chaitanya from the lotus lips of Srila Gaura Kishore Das Babaji Maharaja and from Srila Krishnadas Babaji, who was the personal servant of Srila Bhaktivinoda Thakura. According to the order of Srila Bhaktivinoda Thakura, Badol took *harinama* (first initiation) from Srila Krishnadas Babaji Maharaja, and he accepted Bhaktivinoda Thakura as his *shiksha-guru*. In the year 1900, when he was 16 years old, he manifested the pastime of marriage in order to bring new *sevikas* for Lord Chaitanya's services. As a result, he got two daughters. In 1908, he took second initiation (*diksha*) from Srila Prabhupada when Srila Prabhupada was still a *brahmachari*. Srila Prabhupada sent him to Chatak Parvat in Jagannath Puri. where the present day Purushottam Math is situated. After second initiation, Srila Prabhupada gave him the name Haripada Das Vanachari, as he had left home. When he lived in Chatak Parvat, he would take Jagannath Mahaprasad on a daily

basis, which cost 4 rupees and 50 paisa per month. As
soon as Srila Prabhupada knew about it, he ordered
him, saying, "Whatever you get from begging should
be cooked by your own hands and offered to the Lord
as *bhoga* daily." He followed Srila Prabhupada's order
without argument.

In 1914, when Srila Bhaktivinoda Thakura physically
passed away in Calcutta, Haripada Das Vanachari came
to Bengal and spent several months in Mayapur. In 1918,
Srila Prabhupada took *sannyasa*. In the same year, after a
few months, Srila Prabhupada gave *sannyasa* initiation to
Haripada Das Vanachari, and his name became Tridandi
Swami Srila Bhakti Swarupa Parvat Goswami Maharaja.
After taking *sannyasa*, he visited the four *dhamas* bare feet.

After 30 years of his *sannyasa* initiation, in order
to fulfill the order of Srila Prabhupada, Srila Parvat
Maharaja got an unbelievable donation from the

Kaptipada King of Odisha, including a palace and agriculture land at Udala, Mayurbhanj, Odisha. Srila Parvat Goswami Maharaja installed Srila Prabhupada's holy footprints at that place, thus showing us by example how to keep firm faith in our spiritual master. Eventually, he named the place Sri Varshabhanavi-dayita Gaudiya Math; therein, he established the Bhaktivinoda-vani Prachar Sabha preaching center at Udala, Mayurbhanj, Odisha.

Srila Parvat Maharaja preached mostly in Odisha state. Many people were able to take shelter of Srila Prabhupada through Srila Parvat Maharaja's preaching endeavor. After Srila Prabhupada's physical departure, Srila Parvat Goswami Maharaja became an initiating *guru*. His most prominent disciples were Bhakti Vikash Mahayogi Maharaja, Bhakti Sundar Sagar Goswami Maharaja, Bhakti Prapanna Parivrajak Maharaja (who established a temple near ISKCON in the name of Sri Krishna Chaitanya Gaudiya Math), Giridhari Das Babaji Maharaja, Pranakishore Brahmachari, etc.

In 1957, on the day of Srila Prabhupada's appearance, His Divine Grace Srila Bhakti Swarupa Parvat Goswami Maharaja physically left all of us at Sri Varshabhanavi-devi-dayita Gaudiya Math, Udala, Mayurbhanj, Odisha. His exemplary dedication to the service of Sri Guru, Vaishnava and Bhagavan is the inspiration for all spiritual seekers. If anyone reads his short biography, one will definitely get pure devotion. The characters of pure devotees inspire us to practice pure devotion.

CHAPTER THIRTY-ONE

SRILA BHAKTI VAIBHAVA PURI GOSWAMI MAHARAJA

A transcendental child appeared on 26 January 1913 in the village of Fulta, situated near Berhampur, Ganjam district in Odisha, India. The father, Sri Damodar, and mother, Srimati Devi, named the baby, Nrisimha.

Since childhood, Nrisimha was academically talented and completed his higher education with a B.A. degree from the local college, Khallikote, at Berhampur, Odisha. However, the young boy was interested in the knowledge of Ayurveda. Thus, he went on to study under a famous Ayurvedic doctor named Madhusudan Sharma, who was initiated, along with his wife, by Srila Prabhupada. We know from *Sri Chaitanya-charitamrita* that the root cause of devotion to Krishna is the association of Vaishnavas (pure devotees). Thus, Nrisimha got devotional inspiration from his Ayurveda teacher, Sripad Madhusudan Prabhu. He was fortunately connected to the *guru-parampara* by receiving *harinama* (first initiation) from Srila Prabhupada on 3 August 1936 at Mayapur, Sri Chaitanya Math. After initiation, Srila Prabhupada gave Nrsimha the name Nrisimhananda Prabhu. Subsequently, Nrisimhananda Prabhu received *diksha* (second initiation) in 1937, after Srila Prabhupada's passing away, from one of his reputed senior godbrothers.

Sripad Nrisimhananda Prabhu quickly gained expertise in giving discourses on different scriptural evidence in various languages such as Telegu, Oriya, Hindi, English, etc. He had very sweet relations with and offered due respect to all of his godbrothers. He was therefore appointed

as the temple president of Madras Gaudiya Math and Sri Ramananda Gaudiya Math at Kovvur, Andhra Pradesh.

To spread the loving message of Mahaprabhu in different parts of India as well as abroad, he was inspired to take the vow of renunciation, *sannyasa*. On 7 February 1966, Sripad Nrisimhananda Prabhu took *sannyasa* initiation from his dearmost godbrother Srila Bhakti Sarvasva Giri Goswami Maharaja at Yogapith temple, the birthplace of Lord Sri Chaitanya Mahaprabhu. He was then known as Srila Bhakti Vaibhava Puri Goswami Maharaja.

Eventually, Srila Bhakti Vaibhava Puri Goswami Maharaja established more than 15 centers in India and several centers abroad, such as Sri Radha Govinda Gaudiya Math in Vienna, Austria. Presently, that center is taken care of by one of his disciples, Srila Bhakti Sadhak Muni Maharaja. He also has preaching centers in Italy, Spain, etc., till today. Presently, many of Srila Bhakti Vaibhava Puri Maharaja's qualified disciples, such as Srila Bhakti Vichar Vishnu Maharaja, Bhakti Svarup Sridhar Maharaja, etc., are preaching all over the world.

On 3 March 2009, during evening *Arati* in his center at Vishakhapatnam, Andhra Pradesh, Srila Bhakti Vaibhava Puri Goswami Maharaja physically passed away. It is an absolute truth that, having taken birth in the material world, everyone must die. However, Srila Bhakti Vaibhava Puri Maharaja shall remain immortal in our memories for his exceptional devotional service. His entire life teaches us to become truthful, humble, respectful and forbearing. These are the most important qualities in pure devotional practices.

CHAPTER THIRTY-TWO

Srila Bhaktivedanta Swami Goswami Maharaja

S ri Chaitanya sent many of his eternal associates to spread His loving mission all around the world. One of these extraordinary and exalted personalities took birth on Tuesday, 1 September 1896, on Nandotsava (the day after Janmashtami), at 151 Harrison Road, Calcutta, West Bengal. The boy was born in a family of *suvarna baniks* (gold merchants) and would in the future be known as Srila Bhaktivedanta Swami Goswami Maharaja. His father, Gourmohan De, and mother, Rajani Bala, were Vaishnavas and named their son Abhay Charan. In accordance with Bengali tradition, upon the child's birth, the parents requested an astrologer to prepare his birth chart. The astrologer predicted, "This baby boy has so many symptoms for spreading the loving message of the Supreme Lord; he will also establish many temples around the world." Due to the influence of his parents, Abhay Charan was spiritually inclined and intellectual by nature since childhood.

At a young age, Abhay Charan, along with his friends, arranged a Ratha Yatra festival in his neighborhood. He frequently visited the *Jagannath* Ratha Yatra conducted by the residents of North Calcutta. While attending the Ratha Yatra festival, Abhay Charan had the desire to establish such festivals in the future – decades later, he inaugurated Ratha Yatra festivals across the world. Since his childhood, he would take only the remnants of food offered to the deities and felt a natural attraction to saintly persons.

Abhay Charan studied English, philosophy and economics at the Scottish Church College in Calcutta. In 1918, when Abhay Charan was 22 years old, his marriage was arranged with Radharani, the daughter of his father's business friend. In the same year, Abhay Charan's future spiritual master, Bimala Prasad, had just completed his vow of chanting one billion holy names and took *sannyasa*.

Although marriage is often seen to be in opposition to renunciation, soon after his marriage in 1922, Abhay Charan came in contact with his spiritual master. Abhay Charan and his friend visited the first preaching center of the Gaudiya Math established by Srila Prabhupada in Calcutta.

Upon seeing Srila Prabhupada's divine form, Abhay Charan felt a deep attraction from the bottom of his heart and offered his prostrate obeisance. Srila Prabhupada allowed Abhay Charan and his friend to sit in front of him. Abhay Charan and his friend asked various questions regarding politics and the independence of India from the British. Srila Prabhupada replied, "There is one Supreme Lord, who is Krishna. He is to be served by one and all. All other living entities are Krishna's servants. This is the philosophy of Sri Chaitanya. If anybody is under the trap of illusion (*maya*), running behind the objects of sense enjoyment in a greedy and lusty manner, and they try to establish the government, then their principles will be unstable and always changing. The principles of such people will never be effective in establishing peace in society. Our goal is to reach above this where we can be eternally blissful. You know the English language well. Why don't you spread the message of Lord Chaitanya to the English-speaking world?" Hearing this brief explanation by Srila Prabhupada, Abhay Charan started to think that his own engagement with M. K. Gandhi, Subhash Chandra Bose and other political leaders was not the ultimate goal of life. From that time onward, Abhay Charan deliberated on how to attain the ultimate goal of life.

In order to maintain his householder life, Abhay Charan opened a pharmaceutical business in Prayag. In 1932, Srila Prabhupada went there on a preaching tour along with various *sannyasis, brahmacharis* and other associates. At that time, at the Allahabad Gaudiya Math, Srila Prabhupada gave Abhay Charan both *harinama* and *diksha* (first and second initiations) simultaneously, as well as the name Abhay Charanaravinda Das Adhikari.

In 1935, Srila Prabhupada was at Radha Kunda, Govardhan. Abhay Charanaravinda Das Adhikari Prabhu, along with his son, went there to visit his *gurudeva*. On the banks of Radha Kunda, Srila Prabhupada spoke words to Abhay Charanaravinda Das Adhikari Prabhu that deeply entered his heart. Srila Prabhupada said, "I had a desire to print some books. If you ever get money, print books."

On 1 January 1937 at 5:30 AM, Srila Prabhupada physically departed from this world, leaving behind a very important instruction to all his followers. He said, "Everybody should cooperatively spread the message of Rupa Goswami and Raghunath Das Goswami under the shelter of Srimati Radharani, who is our one and only shelter and the actual *acharya*." (*Acharya* is one who teaches how to serve the Lord in the most precise manner through their own example).

We know from scriptures that whatever a pure devotee instructs will surely manifest. Srila Prabhupada's instruction to Abhay

Charanaravinda Das Adhikari Prabhu at the Gaudiya
Math (No. 1 Ultadingi Junction Road) and at Radha
Kunda gradually manifested in the following ways.

In 1944, Abhay Charanaravinda Das Adhikari
Prabhu established an English magazine called *Back
to Godhead,* wherein he wrote and published articles
on spirituality based on Srila Bhaktivinoda Thakura's
philosophy. Simultaneously, in order to fulfill his
gurudeva's order, Abhay Charanaravinda Das Adhikari
Prabhu started to translate the *Srimad Bhagavad Gita*
into English.

However, as stated in the scriptures – *śreyāṁsi bahu-
vignāni* – performing auspicious activities is always met
with obstacles. Abhay Charanaravinda Das Adhikari
Prabhu contracted tuberculosis. There was no proper
medicine at the time, and his wife and other family
members did not allow him to stay at home, as it was
an infectious disease. The Supreme Lord inspired Srila

re there is Godhead there is no Nescience.

nded (It revives man's Divine nature)
ti Siddhanta Saraswati Goswami Prabhupada
n Bhaktivedanta.

Bhakti Dayita Madhava Goswami Maharaja to bring Abhay Charanaravinda Das Adhikari Prabhu to his temple, Sri Chaitanya Gaudiya Math in Calcutta, and look after him. After six months under the care of Srila Madhava Goswami Maharaja, who arranged for expensive medications and personal care, by the mercy of the Supreme Lord Abhay Charanaravinda Das Adhikari Prabhu was physically healed. After all, the Lord is our actual shelter. This is an example of genuine Vaishnava culture, keeping amicable relations in order to carry forward the loving mission of Sri Chaitanya.

Although Abhay Charanaravinda Das Adhikari Prabhu was endeavoring to fulfill the order of his *gurudeva*, he often faced obstacles from his family life. When his wife, Radharani, sold his copy of *Srimad Bhagavatam* to get money to buy tea, he decided to renounce his household life and went to Vrindavan in

order to completely dedicate himself to fulfilling the orders of his *gurudeva*.

On 17 September 1959, Abhay Charanaravinda Das Adhikari Prabhu took *sannyasa* from his senior godbrother Srila Bhakti Prajnan Keshava Goswami Maharaja, founder of Sri Gaudiya Vedanta Samiti, and received the name Srila Bhaktivedanta Swami Goswami Maharaja. For several years, Srila Bhaktivedanta Swami Goswami Maharaja stayed in a small room at Sri Radha-Damodar temple, which is situated next to Srila Rupa Goswami's *samadhi* in Vrindavan. There, according to the instruction of his *gurudeva*, he chanted 64 rounds of the Hare Krishna *maha-mantra* every day and worked on translating the *Srimad Bhagavad Gita* and *Srimad Bhagavatam* into English.

In 1964, in order to fulfill the desire of his *gurudeva*, he decided to go outside India to preach the loving message of Sri Chaitanya to the English-speaking audience. He got in contact with Scindia shipping company's owner, Sumati Morarjee Desai, and she arranged a room for him on a ship. On 13 August 1965 at 07:00, Srila Bhaktivedanta Swami Goswami Maharaja left on the *Jaladuta* ship from Calcutta to Boston. He

suffered two heart attacks on the journey, but the Lord wanted him to survive to fulfill an important mission. Sri Chaitanya appeared in the form of Krishna to Srila Bhaktivedanta Swami Goswami Maharaja and safely took him to Boston Port on 17 September 1965. He started what would then be an international movement called ISKCON with just a pair of hand cymbals (*karatals*). Eventually, Srila Bhaktivedanta Swami Goswami Maharaja transformed hippies into 'happies' through the chanting of the Hare Krishna *maha-mantra*. Apart from that, he also transformed the lives of students, artists, professors, professional musicians and social workers.

The desire of the exalted personality Srila Prabhupada Bhaktisiddhanta Saraswati Goswami Thakura gradually began to manifest through one of his affectionate disciples, Srila Bhaktivedanta Swami Goswami Maharaja. In 1966, Srila Bhaktivedanta Swami Goswami Maharaja established the International Society for Krishna Consciousness (ISKCON), widely known as the Hare Krishna Movement, in order to spread the loving message of Sri Chaitanya and propagate chanting of the holy names of Krishna. Over time, he met many famous and celebrated personalities, such as George Harrison of the Beatles, Alfred Ford of Ford Motor Company, Allen Ginsberg, and various professors and scholars of top universities. He convinced them about the philosophy of Sri Chaitanya.

Srila Bhaktivedanta Swami Goswami Maharaja spread the Hare Krishna Movement across various countries and established ISKCON centers in dozens of cities throughout the world. One of the most attractive centers at that time was the Bhaktivedanta Manor, which was donated by George Harrison in

England. Through the spiritual potency and instruction of Srila Prabhupada and his selfless devotion, Srila Bhaktivedanta Swami Goswami Maharaja became successful, even at the advanced age of seventy years, in miraculously and rapidly spreading the loving message of Sri Chaitanya all over the world within a span of only twelve years (1965 to 1977).

His preaching strategy included the distribution of devotional books accompanied with congregational chanting of the Hare Krishna *maha-mantra*. He opened centers for establishing unity in diversity. He founded temples, spiritual schools, farm communities, Vaishnava festivals and the Bhaktivedanta Book Trust, which was the *brhad mridanga* that published various scriptures and other literature. One of his major goals was to establish Vedic *daiva-varnashrama* in the western world.

Within a few years of his preaching in America, many people became his followers. Due to his previous amicable relation with Srila Madhava Goswami Maharaja's temple as mentioned above, Srila Bhaktivedanta Swami Goswami Maharaja sent three of his disciples, namely Achyutananda Das Brahmachari, Jayapataka Das Brahmachari (later known as Jayapataka Swami Maharaja) and Bhavananda Das, to Srila Madhava Goswami Maharaja's temple, Sri Chaitanya Gaudiya Math in Calcutta, for further development in Vaishnava etiquette and culture. Eventually, they started the first mission of ISKCON in India at Calcutta. Later on, Srila Bhaktivedanta Swami Goswami Maharaja established ISKCON'S world headquarters at Sridham Mayapur. In order to spread messages throughout India, Srila Bhaktivedanta Swami Goswami Maharaja established ISKCON

centers in various cities of India, including Mumbai, Hyderabad, Vrindavan and so on.

Vaiṣṇavera kriyā, mudrā vijñeha nā bujhaya: the actions of Vaishnavas cannot be understood by even the most expert of scholars. In order to spread the loving message of Sri Chaitanya, Srila Bhaktivedanta Swami Goswami Maharaja sometimes ignored the endeavors of some of his other godbrothers as seen through his instructions and various letters to disciples. On 13 October 1977, Srila Bhakti Vaibhava Puri Goswami Maharaja and others went to visit Srila Bhaktivedanta Swami Goswami Maharaja while he was manifesting sickness pastimes in Vrindavan a month before his departure from this world. At that time, Srila Bhaktivedanta Swami Goswami Maharaja asked for forgiveness from his godbrothers – "Everyone at whose lotus feet I committed offense, please forgive me. I committed offense to the Vaishnavas (*vaishnava-aparadha*) and having gained some opulence, I became proud." At that time, Srila Bhakti Vaibhava Puri Goswami Maharaja stated, "Through your preaching the Hare Krishna *maha-mantra*, opulence ran behind you. That is the wealth of Krishna. You preached and expanded the devotees, which is the desire of Srila Prabhupada and Mahaprabhu. This is the actuality. Where is the offense (*aparadh*)? Everything is auspicious. There is no offense."

This conversation establishes the true Vaishnava mood, avoiding antagonism with anyone. Srila Bhaktivedanta Swami Goswami Maharaja established the real mood of

CHAPTER THIRTY-THREE

SRILA BHAKTI VICHAR JAJABAR GOSWAMI MAHARAJA

People are born all over the world, but fortunate souls are always directed by the Supreme Lord to the place for the ultimate eternal benefit. One personality amongst those eternally perfect associates is Srila Bhakti Vichar Jajabar Goswami Maharaja, whose eternal identity is Malati Manjari in the spiritual world.

Srila Jajabar Goswami Maharaja's family members were originally *brahmana* servitors of Viraja Devi in Sri Jagannath Puri Dham. After some time, the family moved to the Durmuth village located in Kanthi district of East Medinipur, West Bengal. On 1 May 1908 (18 Vaishakh 1315), the day of *Akshaya Dvitiya* (day before Akshaya Tritiya, when Chandan Yatra starts), an effulgent *brahmana* boy was born to Padmalochan Sharma and Srimati Rukmini Devi, When the baby was still in Srimati Rukmini Devi's womb, she often had dreams about the pastimes of Sri Krishna in Vrindavan. This was an indication that the child would be an exalted devotee (*mahapurush*). Thus, the parents and family members named the baby Sarveshwar Panda. Sarveshwar is a name of the Supreme Lord Krishna, which means the Lord of all Lords.

Since childhood, Sarveshwar was simple, enthusiastic, and hardworking. He was inclined towards renunciation. At a very young age, following the desire of his father he memorized all the verses of the *Srimad Bhagavad Gita*. His relatives inspired him to join the Ramakrishna Mission's *Belur Math* near Calcutta. Sarveshwar went to *Belur Math*, where he lived for some time. When he realized that the residents there were consuming non-vegetarian food, he immediately left the Belur Math and continued his search for the spiritual path that would give him fulfilment and a genuine seer of the truth.

At the age of 18, Sarveshwar secretly left home for Jagannath Puri *dhama* in search of a spiritual master. Upon arrival in Puri, he resided at the home of a priest of Lord Jagannath. One day, as he was returning to his residence after a bath in the ocean, Sarveshwar met with a *sannyasi* begging for alms. He was Bhakti Prasun Bodhayan Goswami Maharaja, a disciple of Srila Prabhupada. Sarveshwar offered his obeisance and whatever he had with him to Srimad Bhakti Prasun Bodhayan Goswami Maharaja The *sannyasi* asked Sarveshwar about his background. Sarveshwar expressed that he was searching for a pure devotee of the Lord under whom he could take shelter. Srila Bodhayan Goswami Maharaja immediately invited Sarveshwar to the Gaudiya Math located at Chatak Parvat, Jagannath Puri to meet with Srila Prabhupada.

In 1926, by the unlimited mercy of Sri Jagannathdeva, Sarveshwar made his way to Sri Purushottam Math located at Chatak Parvat where he had his first *darshan* of Srila Prabhupada. He was enamored by Srila Prabhupada's tall, effulgent, grave form and personality. Sarveshwar desperately explained to Srila Prabupada his intense desire to see the Supreme Lord. Srila Prabhupada became extremely joyful, kept Sarveshwar in his close association for some days and personally explained topics on the Supreme Absolute Truth to him. Sarveshwar then realized that this was the spiritual master whom he was earnestly seeking and decided to surrender wholeheartedly to Srila Prabhupada's divine feet.

On the auspicious day of Gaura Purnima that same year, Srila Prabhupada gave Sarveshwar *harinama* and *diksha* (first and second initiation) along with Sri Radha *mantra*. His new name became Sarveshwar Das Brahmachari. After initiation, Srila Prabhupada observed his nature and realized that he would be a good *pujari*. He therefore engaged him as a *pujari* for the deities at Sri Chaitanya Math, Sridham Mayapur (Sri Sri Guru Gauranga Gandharvika Giridhari).

Srila Prabhupada also engaged him in studying Sanskrit grammar through Jiva Goswami's *Harinammrta Vyakarana* in the temple campus' Sanskrit school. Sarveshwar Brahmachari focused on his study and *puja* without wasting any time on excessive sleep or useless gossip. Seeing Sarveshwar Brahmachari's inclinations and nature, Srila Prabhupada engaged him in various services in different temples, such as in Calcutta, Dhaka, Patna, Gaya, Kashi, Prayag, Kurukshetra, etc.

Once, the Gaudiya Math was invited to an International Religious Conference in Calcutta and Srila Prabhupada chose Sarveshwar Brahmachari to present the philosophy of the Gaudiya Math in that conference. Sarveshwar Brahmachari was not very educated in terms of material academics and therefore felt so fearful to bear such a huge responsibility that he began crying. He felt unqualified to represent the Gaudiya Math in that huge conference. He requested Srila Prabhupada's personal servant, Sripad Krishnananda Prabhu, to request Prabhupada to engage someone who was more educated to attend the conference, such as Srila Bhakti Rakshak Sridhar Goswami, Srila Bhakti Hridaya Bon Goswami, Sripad Atul Chandra Prabhu, etc. As soon as Sripad Krishnananda Prabhu presented this message to Srila Prabhupada, Srila Prabhupada said, "Why is he crying? There can be no change. He should follow whatever I have said." With eyes full of tears, Sarveshwar Brahmachari went to the conference.

The next day, Srila Prabhupada was reading the newspaper and the headline read, "Glories of the Gaudiya Math." Sarveshwar Brahmachari had so brilliantly presented the teachings of the Gaudiya Math. Srila Prabhupada called all of his disciples who were present and said, "Look. He was crying and felt unqualified but now look at his qualification. Actually, we are all unqualified, but we become qualified when we receive the mercy of the *guru-parampara*. We are not representing Mahaprabhu's mission by our academic degrees. It is actually Mahaprabhu's mercy which allows us to represent His mission."

Once, Sarveshwar Das Brahmachari went to Dhaka, Bangladesh with Srila Prabhupada. A miraculous incident took place. There was a landlord (*zamindar*) who was by nature completely atheistic. If people did not follow what he liked, he would punish them by physically beating them. When Srila Prabhupada reached that place, the local people informed Srila Prabhupada about him. Srila Prabhupada sent Sarveshwar Brahmachari to the house of the landlord to beg alms, but the wife of the landlord very roughly rejected Sarveshwar Brahmachari. This incident recurred over several days. Then one day, the wife of the landlord gave Sarveshwar Brahmachari some uncooked rice. He took that rice back to the temple. The next day, he cooked it in the temple and brought the *prasadam* (blessed remnants) of the cooked rice along with other preparations back to the landlord's house. A while after this incident, the atheistic landlord's family all became disciples of Srila Prabhupada. This incident illustrates the power of *mahaprasad* and *sukriti* (pious credit) obtained from serving Vaishnavas, even if its unwillingly or unknowingly.

In 1935, the Gaudiya Math in Gaya was facing problems as the local people refused to cooperate with the temple. Srila Prabhupada sent Sarveswhar Prabhu to Gaya and due to the influence of his purity and character, the entire atmosphere transformed, and all of the local residents became inspired to cooperate with the temple again.

While Sarveshwar Das Brahmachari was in Bag Bazaar Gaudiya Math, he once met with his relatives. This was 12 years after he had taken up renounced life, staying at the Gaudiya Math. He brought his relatives to meet Srila Prabhupada. Thereafter, Srila Prabhupada told Sarveshwar Das Brahmachari to return with his relatives and preach in their home.

In 1936, during a spiritual meeting (Navadwip Dham Pracharini Sabha) conducted at the Yogapith temple, Mayapur, in the presence of Srila Prabhupada, Sarveshwar Prabhu sweetly chanted *kirtan* and gave discourses with attractive Vaishnava language. Thereafter, Srila Prabhupada gave him the title 'Ragaratna' (jewel of spontaneous loving devotion) and gave him the Bhakti Shastri certificate. Thus, he was known as Ragaratna Sarveshwar Brahmachari Bhakti Shastri.

krsna-mantra haite habe samsāra-mocana
krsna-nāma haite pābe krsnera carana

"Through chanting the Krishna Mantra, one gets released from all material attachments. By chanting the holy name of Krishna, one attains the divine lotus feet of Krishna."

This verse always resounded within Sarveshwar Brahmachari's ears. One must perform the spiritual practice of chanting the mantra, or there will be destruction of the body. A lion cannot think that a deer will automatically enter into its mouth if it is sleeping and not actively hunting (*na hi suptasya simhasya pravisanti mukhe mrgah*). Thus, he would lovingly chant the *mana-mantra* with great enthusiasm, chanting at least 100,000 names of Krishna (64 rounds) every day. This practice of chanting 64 rounds started when he joined the Gaudiya

Math as a *brahmachari* and never stopped, even when he was physically ill.

Sarveshwar Brahmachari also sang the *kirtans* of previous Gaudiya Vaishnava *acharyas* and worshiped and served the deities of the Lord. He served his godbrothers with extreme dedication and sincerity.

Srila Prabhupada was extremely pleased with Sarveshwar Brahmachari's mood. Srila Prabhupada loved listening to the *kirtans* that he would sing so sweetly. In 1936, Srila Prabhupada gave him the spiritual title 'Sarveshwarananda Ragaratna' (the jewel of musical melodies who gives bliss to the Lord of one and all).

Sarveshwar Brahmachari served as a *math-rakshak* (in a management capacity) at four *maths,* in Patna, Prayag, Kashi, and Gaya. He preached the spiritual philosophical conclusions of Sri Sri Guru and Gauranga by reading from scriptures, singing *kirtans* and giving discourses. He studied *Harinammrta Vyakarana* (Sanskrit grammar book in which all the technical terms in the *sutras* are names of Krishna or his associates) and many spiritual scriptures. While he was the *math-rakshak* at Gaya, many scholars saw Sarveshwar Brahmachari's expertise and became attracted, thereby receiving mercy and gaining the shelter of Srila Prabhupada's divine lotus feet.

Srila Prabhupada became extremely pleased with Sarveshwar Brahmachari and on his own decided to grant Sarveshwar Brahmachari *sannyasa* (renounced order). Srila Prabhupada called him to Purushottam Math located in Chatak Parvat, Jagannath Puri during the Ratha Yatra festival and gave him *sannyasa* initiation at the mere age of 27. He received the name Srila Bhakti Vichar Jajabar Maharaja, and he was the last person to whom Srila Prabhupada gave *sannyasa.*

Srila Jajabar Goswami Maharaja was not only an excellent *kirtan* singer; he possessed all the qualities of

a Vaishnava. By the grace of Srila Prabhupada, Srila Jajabar Goswami Maharaja was well versed in all facets of Vaishnava philosophy and used to disseminate these teachings in simple and eloquent language using *Srimad Bhagavatam* and *Srimad Bhagavad Gita* as a basis.

In the Conference of World Religions at Rangoon (currently known as Yangoon, in Mayanmar), he presented the inner meaning of the science of consciousness from the *Vedas* (*sanatana dharma*) in an understandable way and attracted the minds of everyone there. The professors of Varanasi University did not accept Sri Chaitanya Mahaprabhu as the source of incarnations (*avatari*). Then, Srila Jajabar Goswami Maharaja wrote a book called *Avatara Samiksha* explaining the incarnations of the Supreme Lord and sent it to the university through his disciple who was a scholar. In this way, he liberated the university professors from the concept of impersonalism (*nirvisesa-vada*) and established pure devotion (*suddha bhakti*).

In 1937, after Srila Prabhupada's physical departure, Srila Jajabar Goswami Maharaja's peaceful, sweet and simple nature kept him away from conflict and inspired him to establish a temple named Shyamananda Gaudiya Math along with like-minded godbrothers in Medinipur. Thereafter he established several other *maths*. Previously, he had also established a temple in Mayapur, named Sri Chaitanya Bhagavat Math, as well as a temple in Jagannath Puri.

Srila Jajabar Goswami Maharaja's life was filled with miracles. Once he, along with his disciples, went to the home of one of his *sannyasi* disciples for preaching. When Srila Jajabar Goswami Maharaja reached that home with his disciples, a snake had bitten one of their neighbors. Srila Jajabar Goswami Maharaja along with his disciples went to that house and read the pastimes of Lord Krishna subduing the Kaliya snake (*Kaliya-daman*) from *Srimad Bhagavatam*. After hearing Srila Jajabar Goswami Maharaja's recitation of the *Kaliya-daman* pastimes, the neighbor that was bitten by the snake was miraculously cured, got up and offered his obeisance to Srila Jajabar Goswami Maharaja.

For a long time, until the age of 78, Srila Jajabar Goswami Maharaja performed many transcendental pastimes in the material world. On the morning of the anniversary day of Srila Narottam Das Thakura's disappearance, Srila Jajabar Goswami Maharaja was severely ill, but he was completely calm, quiet and conscious. All of the disciples surrounding him were chanting the Hare Krishna *maha-mantra*, and Srila Jajabar Goswami Maharaja was also chanting with his soft voice. That evening, Srila Jajabar Goswami Maharaja physically departed from this world from Shyamananda Gaudiya Math in Medinipur. The date was 15 October 1984 (Bengali calendar: 28 Ashwin 1391) at 17:30. He departed in the presence of his disciples and his appointed successor, Bhakti Vistar Vishnu Goswami Maharaja.

During the disappearance pastime, Bhakti Vistar Vishnu Goswami Maharaja saw in his divine vision a beautiful, transcendental chariot in which Sri Sri Radha Krishna were seated on a beautiful throne; two *sakhis* appeared from that chariot in front of Srila Jajabar Goswami Maharaja, and they said, "This is our Malati Manjari", and they took him to the spiritual world. After his physical departure, his disciples decided to take Srila Jajabar Goswami Maharaja's holy transcendental body to Sri Mayapur Dham, and he was placed in *samadhi* at his Sri Chaitanya Bhagavat Math.

Srila Jajabar Goswami Maharaja's entire spiritual life teaches us to keep sound faith in the words of the spiritual master and the authentic scriptures. Eventually, the eternal truth will be revealed in our hearts; there is no need to depend upon academic degrees. We just need the blessings of the *parampara* in order to reach our ultimate destination – Sri Goloka Vrindavan.

Srila Prabhupada said that Bhakti Vichar Jajabar Maharaja is an embodiment of Mahaprabhu's service mission.

CHAPTER THIRTY-FOUR

SRILA BHAKTI VIJAY SAGAR GOSWAMI MAHARAJA

His Divine Grace Srila Bhaktisiddhanta Saraswati Goswami Thakura Prabhupada's magnanimity was nondifferent from Lord Chaitanya's. Srila Bhakti Vijay Sagar Goswami Maharaja was a spiritual descendant of Srila Prabhupada and Lord Chaitanya. On Guru Purnima, Friday, 6 July 1906 (22 Ashadh 1313), Srila Sagar Goswami Maharaja appeared in Khulna, Bangladesh. He was the only son of his parents, Kartik Chandra Sarkar and Charulata Devi. They lovingly named him Jitendranath, the conqueror of all the senses.

In his discourses, Srila Prabhupada often said, "I am not accepting any disciples. Rather, I am accepting *gurus*. Whoever practices spirituality are all my deliverers from the upcoming material dangers (*vipada-uddharana-band-hava*)." Jitendranath's birthday (Guru Purnima) was an indication that he would be a *guru* in Mahaprabhu's lineage. Once, when Jitendranath was a little boy, he saw a devotional drama called *Vijay Vasanta*. After that, he felt detachment from material life.

In order to pull Jitendranath out of his material life to a renounced life, Lord Chaitanya arranged a connection through one of his neighbors who was a disciple of Srila Prabhupada. Once, Jitendranath asked his neighbor, "What is the use of taking vegetarian food?" The devotee neighbor explained the benefit of accepting *prasadam*. When Jitendranath was 16 years old, he left home and came to Sridham Mayapur, taking shelter of the lotus feet of his *gurudeva*, Srila Prabhupada. Srila Prabhupada was happy to see Jitendranath's austere service mood. In a short space of time, Srila Prabhupada gave him *harinama* and *diksha* (first and second initiation) and named him Sri Yamalarjuna-bhanjana Brahmachari.

By nature, Yamalarjuna-bhanjana Brahmachari was soft, humble and enthusiastic to serve all the Vaishnavas. Therefore, everybody liked him. Srila Prabhupada sent him in the preaching field under the guidance of senior *sannyasis*. All *sannyasis* liked his nature and engaged him in various services at the temples where he went.

After Srila Prabhupada's physical departure in 1937, Yamalarjuna-bhanjana Brahmachari felt intense separation. At that time, Srila Prabhupada appeared in his dream and gave him an instruction – "Don't feel insecure. I am always with you and everyone in spirit." The dream reassured Yamalarjuna-bhanjana Brahmachari and he again felt enthusiasm to spread the loving mission of Lord Chaitanya under the shelter of Sri Chaitanya Math (Adi-math). Yamalarjuna-bhanjana Prabhu visited almost all pilgrimage places in India and was inspired to take *sannyasa* initiation.

In 1948, Yamalarjuna-bhanjana Prabhu took *sannyasa* from Srila Bhakti Prakash Aranya Goswami Maharaja and received the name Tridandi Swami Bhakti Vijay Sagar Goswami Maharaja. After *sannyasa* initiation, Srila Sagar Maharaja established *maths* (preaching centers) in Durgapur and Asansol, West Bengal. Due to lack of assistance in running these temples, he left the two temples without any hesitation and went to Chaitanya Math again. During his stay at Chaitanya Math, he also established a temple in Godrumadvipa, Swarup Ganj. However, he felt that he was not eligible to run temples and therefore offered the temple to his senior godbrother His Divine Grace Srila Bhakti Vilas Tirtha Goswami Maharaja.

Significant time passed, and following several requests from his disciples, Srila Sagar Goswami Maharaja again established a temple in the name of Sri Rupanuga Gaudiya Math at Nandipara (Hospital More), Sridham Mayapur, Nadia. By nature, Maharaja was free from material belongings and attachments (*nishkincan*). If anybody offered him financial support, he often replied,

"Too much opulence is the cause of our distress. Whenever I need any financial support, I will ask you." Too much money in the hands of a renounced person is not favorable for practicing devotion, as it increases material opulence. Thus, Srila Sagar Goswami Maharaja used to refuse many financial donations.

Srila Sagar Goswami Maharaja would cordially attend all invitations from the temples in Mayapur. He also attended all festivals with full humility. I have seen, several times, that he came to attend the appearance day festival of my spiritual master, His Divine Grace Bhakti Pramode Puri Goswami Maharaja. He frequently visited my spiritual master along with his disciples. One of the disciples was Satya Bhagavat Prabhu (later known as Satya Bhagavat Das Babaji Maharaja). Presently, Sripad Narottama Das Babaji Maharaja is running Sri Rupanuga Gaudiya Math, Mayapur under the guidance of Satya Bhagavat Das Babaji Maharaja.

Srila Sagar Goswami Maharaja physically left all of us at 04:40 on Saturday, 18 May 2002 (3 Jyestha 1409) from his Mayapur temple, Sri Rupanuga Gaudiya Math. Srila Sagar Goswami Maharaja's exemplary devotional practice teaches us to be soft and humble, to respect everyone, and to not be greedy for mundane wealth, which is a most important quality to practice pure devotion. If anyone attentively reads Maharaja's life history, he will surely get inspiration for practicing pure devotion.

CHAPTER THIRTY-FIVE

SRILA BHAKTI VIJNANA ASHRAM GOSWAMI MAHARAJA

One ray of Srila Prabhupada descended from the lotus feet of Lord Chaitanya in 1881, appearing in a *brahmana* Chattopadhyay family in Batika village, Faridpur district, Bangladesh. The boy's parents, Gangadhar Chattopadhyay and Bidhumukhi Devi, named their son Mahendranath Chattopadhyay. From a young age, the boy's nature was unusually saintly, calm and quiet, and thus surrounding people gave him the nickname "Sadhu". Mahendranath was the third of Gangadhar's four sons. All the sons were academically qualified and received higher education degrees.

In line with Bengali tradition, his mother arranged Mahendranath's marriage when he was very young. After finishing his academic degree, Mahendranath worked at the railway and at a steamer company. Later on, he qualified with a degree in homeopathic medicine and practiced as a homeopathic doctor in Guwahati, Assam. Although he was materially successful, Mahendranath remained detached from his profession and education. He kept searching for a higher spiritual purpose in life.

One day, Mahendranath left everything and went on pilgrimage in Uttarakhand to Kedarnath, Badrinath, etc. From there, he went to Calcutta to a Ramakrishna mission preaching center where Mahendranath Gupta, the author of *Sri Ramakrishna Kathamrita,* was living. Mahendranath Gupta was the director of Morton School in Calcutta; he engaged Mahendranath Chattopadhyay (Sadhu) as a teacher in the school. During this time, Sadhu took initiation from *Belur Math* and met Sarada Ma, the wife of Sri Ramakrishna. However, he still did not find inner peace. Mahendranath Chattopadhyay was searching for a higher taste in spiritual practice.

Once, walking along a main road in Calcutta, he saw a sign which read *Gaudiya*. Sadhu was curious to know what the meaning of the word *Gaudiya* was.

He approached various people and found out that the *Gaudiya* was the title of a magazine; he also heard various other explanations but was not clear on what the word meant. One day, Sadhu met with a renounced devotee who was distributing the *Gaudiya* magazine. He found out that that renounced person was from a society called the Gaudiya Math. After some time, Sadhu went on a college trip to Pareshnath Mandir; on the way back, he saw the Gaudiya Math located at No. 1 Ultadingi Junction Road. He and his friend entered and saw the deities of Sri Sri Guru Gauranga Radha Vinodakanta and met with a devotee named Yashodanandan Bhagavat Bhushan. They listened to a discourse on Lord Hari from him and found out that the founder of the Gaudiya Math, Srila Prabhupada, had gone to Dhaka, Bangladesh for some preaching programs.

Sadhu and his friend were inspired and wanted to visit again. After some days, they returned to the Gaudiya Math and fortunately, at that time, Srila Prabhupada was present. As soon as Mahendranath Chattopadhyay saw Srila Prabhupada's divine, effulgent form, a special feeling overwhelmed his heart. Srila Prabhupada asked Mahendranath, "Amongst the 330 million gods and goddesses, who is the supreme?" Srila Prabhupada continued, quoting a verse from the *Sri Brahma Samhita*, *īsvarah paramah krsnah sac-cid-ānanda-vigrahah anādir ādir govindah sarva-kārana-kāranam* – "The Supreme Lord is Sri Krishna, also known as Sri Govinda, who is the embodiment of eternality, cognizance and bliss; He is the origin of all origins and the cause of all causes". Thereafter, Srila Prabhupada quoted a verse from the *Srimad Bhagavatam, ete cāmśa-kalāh pumsah krsnas tu bhagavān svayam* – "The Supreme Lord is Sri Krishna and all parts, expansions and incarnations originate from Him". Sadhu was amazed to hear all of this and began visiting Srila

Prabhupada every day to listen to his discourses even though he was initiated in *Belur Math*. Whilst he was in Calcutta, his wife got pneumonia and passed away. After that, Mahendranath handed over his son and daughter to his elder brother and left his teaching job to completely dedicate himself to the spiritual path.

He visited the birthplaces of Krishna, Ramachandra and Chaitanya Mahaprabhu. When visiting Mahaprabhu's birthplace, Mahendranath stayed at a relative's home in Navadwip town. The next day, he crossed the Ganga by boat and walked along the mud road until he reached Yogapith temple, Sri Mayapur Dham at 1 pm. The temple doors were closed by that time. Hearing that Srila Prabhupada was at Sri Chaitanya Math, which was a little further along the mud road from Yogapith temple, Mahendranath immediately went to Sri Chaitanya Math. Srila Prabhupada was sitting in his *bhajan kutir* and giving dictation of his *Anubhashya* commentary on the *Sri Chaitanya-charitamrita*. As soon as Srila Prabhupada saw Mahendranath, who had walked since the morning in the hot sun, he instructed a *brahmachari* from the *math* to give Mahendranath some *prasadam*.

After taking *prasadam*, Mahendranath took permission from Srila Prabhupada to visit the other holy places such as Advaita Bhavan, Srivas Angan and Yogapith. Mahendranath took rest overnight at Yogapith temple. The next morning, Kirtanananda Brahmachari, who was Srila Prabhupada's personal servant, requested Mahendranath to immediately go to Chaitanya Math. Mahendranath went to Sri Chaitanya Math, and Srila Prabhupada ordered him, "Shave your head and take a bath in the Ganga. Then, come to me wearing fresh clothes." Mahendranath did as instructed. Then, Srila Prabhupada gave him *harinama* and *diksha* (first and second initiation), saffron robes and the new name Mohanamurali

Das Adhikari. He sent Mohanamurali Prabhu to Champatti Gaura Gadadhar temple located in Ritudvipa.

Shortly thereafter, observing Mohanamurali Prabhu's saintly nature, Srila Prabhupada gave him *sannyasa* (renounced order), and he received the name Srila Bhakti Vijnan Ashram Maharaja. According to the order of Srila Prabhupada, Srila Ashram Goswami Maharaja served in Sri Chaitanya Math and Yogapith temple located in Mayapur, Baliati Gadai Gauranga Math located in Bangladesh, Sri Madras Gaudiya Math located in Chennai, and so on. Srila Ashram Goswami Maharaja was engaged in serving as a *pujari* (priest) and in giving discourses on devotional scriptures in all of the places where he served. He used to write many articles; and later on, published two books, namely *Bhakta Charita* and *Chaitanya Lilamrita*. During Srila Prabhupada's manifest pastimes and as per his desire, Srila Ashram Goswami Maharaja was once engaged as the chairman of the Navadwip Dham Pracharini Sabha on Gaura Purnima day in Yogapith temple, wherein various speakers would glorify Sri Chaitanya Mahaprabhu.

Ten years after Srila Prabhupada's physical departure, Kunjabihari Vidyabhushan Prabhu decided to take *sannyasa* in order to continue Srila Prabhupada's mission. Although he was senior to Srila Ashram Goswami Maharaja, due to his simple and saintly nature Kunjabihari Vidyabhushan Prabhu chose to take *sannyasa* from Srila Ashram Goswami Maharaja. The ceremony took place on the day of Gaura Purnima, and Kunjabihari Vidyabhushan Prabhu received the name Srila Bhakti Vilas Tirtha Goswami Maharaja.

Srila Ashram Goswami Maharaja and Srila Bhakti Dayita Madhava Goswami Maharaja were dear friends and often preached together in different places, such as Assam. After Srila Prabhupada's disappearance, Srila

Ashram Goswami Maharaja stayed at Govardhan for an extended period of time, engaging in spiritual practice. Towards the end of his life, he moved to Sri Chaitanya Math and spent his days in spiritual practice, staying in Srila Prabhupada's *bhajan kutir*. On 22 July 1967, the day after Guru Purnima (Bengali calendar 5 Shravan 1374), Srila Ashram Goswami Maharaja entered into the eternal pastimes of Sri Sri Radha-Govinda at 05:00 at the age of 86. His body was placed in *samadhi* at Srivas Angan. On the next day, Sri Chaitanya Math, Mayapur and Sri Chaitanya Gaudiya Math, Calcutta both arranged disappearance festivals according to the Vaishnava tradition, commemorating Srila Bhakti Vijnana Ashram Goswami Maharaja.

CHAPTER THIRTY-SIX

SRILA BHAKTI VILAS GABHASTINEMI GOSWAMI MAHARAJA

Lord Chaitanya is actually the Supreme Personality of Godhead, Sri Krishna. One significant spiritual descendant of Lord Chaitanya is Srila Bhakti Vilas Gabhastinemi Goswami Maharaja. More than 300 years ago, a family of landowners headed by Ramakrishna Sarkar lived in Bhurseet Brahman Para (present-day Maju near Munshirhat, Howrah). Ramakrishna's grandson was Advaita Sarkar, whose son was Srila Nemi Maharaja. At birth, he was given the name Girindranath Sarkar.

Maharaja was a talented student who studied until class 10. Nowadays, people have a misconception that marriage life is not suitable for spiritual practice. In order to break that thought process, at an early age, Maharaja got married to Dhirabala Basurani from Dakshindi, Hooghly, West Bengal. Srila Nemi Maharaja set an example of how to establish a householder devotee family. In order to maintain his family, he worked in an important government department. Simultaneously, he continued to worship his family Giridhari deity.

Maharaja's life reminds us of the instruction that Chaitanya Mahaprabhu gave to Raghunath Das Goswami: *yathā-yogya viṣaya bhuñja' anāsakta hañā* – "give all respect to family duties and simultaneously follow the spiritual practice." Mahaprabhu further explained to Raghunath Das Goswami: *acirāt kṛṣṇa tomāya karibe uddhāra* – "Krishna will soon deliver you from your material family." Maharaja's life was teaching us such an example.

In India, government jobs are sought after. Although Girindranath had a government job and a loyal wife, he was not bound in his family life. He established an *ashram* on his own land and lived there as a renounced person. At the time, Srila Prabhupada came to Brahmana Para with his preaching team. After hearing Srila Prabhupada's *harikatha*, Girindranath was so impressed that, without hesitation, he took shelter of Srila Prabhupada. He took *harinama* and *diksha* (first and second initiation) along with his wife. He received the name Gaura Govinda Das Adhikari, and his wife was named Dhanistha Devi.

Srila Prabhupada soon installed a six-armed Gauranga Murti in Gaura Govinda Das Adhikari's *ashram* and named the *ashram* Sri Sri Prapannashram. After a few years, Srila Prabhupada observed Gaura Govinda Das Adhikari's dedicated service mood and gave him *sannyasa* (renounced order) at Bag Bazar Gaudiya Math; his name became Sri Bhakti Vilas Gabhastinemi Maharaja. Srila Gabhastinemi Maharaja's sweet, melodious *kirtan* and preaching strategy made him dear to Srila Prabhupada.

Once, Srila Prabhupada needed Rs. 500 urgently. In order to fulfill Srila Prabhupada's desire, Srila Gabhastinemi Maharaja took one of his younger godbrothers, Radharaman Das Brahmachari (later known as Bhakti Kumud Santa Goswami Maharaja), and went out for collecting funds. They arrived at a Marwadi businessman's home, but the guard prevented their entry. Maharaja went to the city, hired a car and went back to the house; this time, the guard allowed them to enter. When they entered, they were requested to wait in the guest room. Eventually, the master of the house came with an angry face and requested Maharaja to get out from his home. Maharaja said, "I will leave your home, no problem. But before I go, I would like to tell you the glories of Lord Hari. I would like you to hear the glories of Lord Hari." Immediately, Maharaja began to speak *harikatha* to all there. After Maharaja's melodious and logical scriptural discourse, the Marwadi businessman was impressed and gave Maharaja a donation of Rs. 500. Eventually, all members of that Marwadi businessman's family came to Bag Bazar Gaudiya Math to take shelter of Srila Prabhupada. This incident demonstrates Srila

Nemi Maharaja's perseverance to fulfill his *gurudeva*'s wishes, and his charisma in preaching.

After Srila Prabhupada's physical departure, Srila Nemi Maharaja, out of separation, was not feeling enthusiastic to preach anymore and decided to continue his life in solitary *bhajan* at Sri Sri Prapannashram. There, he established Sri Sri Radha-Govinda deities, served the deities and gave daily discourses with *kirtan*. During his time at Brahman Para, the temple atmosphere was most appealing, and several people frequented the *ashram*. To deliver these people, Srila Nemi Maharaja became an initiating guru and granted several of them initiation.

On Tuesday, 26 April 1938 (13 Vaishakh 1345) at 07:00, this ray of Srila Prabhupada, Srila Bhakti Vilas Gabhastinemi Goswami Maharaja, physically left us. Upon his physical departure, the news spread and many of Srila Prabhupada's disciples from various places came to offer their obeisance and attend the disappearance ceremony. Throughout his life, he maintained an outstanding service attitude and left us with teachings on how to dedicate our lives for the service of Sri Guru, Vaishnava and Bhagavan.

CHAPTER THIRTY-SEVEN

SRILA BHAKTI VILAS TIRTHA GOSWAMI MAHARAJA

Srila Bhakti Vilas Tirtha Goswami Maharaja appeared on Monday, 4 February 1894 (Bengali calendar – 19 Chaitra 1302, Shukla Saptami, 7th day of the waxing-moon cycle) in Chanchuri Purulia village, Narail district, Jessore, Bangladesh. He was born into a Vaishnava family and his father, Ramacharan Das, named him Umapati. As per Vaishnava tradition, after six months an *annaprasana* ceremony was held, during which the baby is fed grains for the first time and is tested for its natural inclination (*ruci-pariksa*). During this ceremony, Umapati picked the *Srimad Bhagavatam*, indicating his spiritual inclination, which manifested in him closely assisting Srila Prabhupada.

In 1911, Umapati passed his secondary school exams. Due to the passing on of his father and the poor financial condition of the family, Umapati was unable to continue his higher education. He found a job at Calcutta General Post Office through which he could financially support his family. While working in Calcutta, he met with a great spiritual personality (*phakir-veshi*). After meeting this person, Umapati was inspired to find a genuine spiritual master. He visited several spiritual institutions in search of a genuine spiritual master. In 1915, on the day of Srila Gaura Kishore Das Babaji Maharaja's disappearance, on the banks of the Ganges, Umapati heard the glories of Lord Hari from Bimala Prasad (who would later be known as Srila Prabhupada Bhaktisiddhanta Saraswati Goswami Thakura). In the same year, Umapati, along with his family, took shelter of Bimala Prasad.

Umapati received the name Kunjabihari Das. After initiation, Kunjabihari Prabhu used to offer his full income to Srila Prabhupada, who would maintain Kunjabihari Prabhu's family. As directed by Srila Prabhupada, Kunjabihari Prabhu began to study various Vedic philosophies (*darshan-shastra*). Pleased with his studies, Srila Prabhupada gave him the title 'Acharyatrik Mahamahopadeshak' Sri Kunjabihari Vidyabhushan Bhagavatratna, which means he was a jewel amongst great spiritual advisors and pure devotees and the ornament of divine knowledge. In 1918, when Srila Prabhupada completed his vow of chanting one billion holy names (*sata-koti-nama-yajna*) and established Sri Chaitanya Math at Mayapur, Sri Kunjabihari Vidyabhushan requested that he come to Calcutta to spread the loving message of Lord Chaitanya at the Bhaktivinoda-asana, located at Ultadingi Junction Road. This was the first preaching center in the city of Calcutta.

During this time, while trying to maintain the services of *guru* and Vaishnavas, Kunjabihari Prabhu was put into much financial debt. He went out of Bengal to earn money in order to pay back his debt. On the order of Srila Prabhupada, Kunjabihari Prabhu came back and engaged his life in spreading the loving message of Lord Chaitanya. In a short period of time, many pious, intelligent people from various places came and took shelter of Srila Prabhupada. Even the extremely miserly Jagadish Babu took shelter of Srila Prabhupada and sponsored the entire construction of the Bag Bazar Gaudiya Math. At the time, the *sannyasis* and *brahmacharis* of the Gaudiya Math used to address Kunjabihari Vidyabhushan as Kunja Da or Kunja Babu. He was the administrator of the Gaudiya Math. Once, Srila Prabhupada expressed, "All glories to Sriman Kunjabihari Vidyabhushan! If his assistants can follow in his footsteps, they will attain great auspiciousness." In brief, we can say that Kunja Da was the embodiment of *guru-seva* and was one who was most dear to his *guru*.

Once, Srila Prabhupada had severe stomach pain. The assistants surrounding Srila Prabhupada applied a hot pack on his stomach, but there was no benefit.

Srila Bhakti Hridaya Bon Goswami Maharaja decided to call Kunja Babu. As soon as Kunja Babu arrived in the room, Srila Prabhupada embraced Kunja Babu and was miraculously cured from the severe pain. Also, in the *Gaudiya* magazine, there is much glorification of Kunja Babu by Bhakti Hridaya Bon Goswami Maharaja, Bhakti Pradipa Tirtha Goswami Maharaja, Sripad Sundarananda Prabhu, Sripad Ananta Vasudeva Prabhu, Sripad Pranavananda Prabhu, Bhakti Rakshak Sridhar Goswami Maharaja and others. Srila Kunjabihari Vidyabhushan followed in the footsteps of Srila Prabhupada at every step in life.

Twelve years after Srila Prabhupada's physical disappearance, Kunjabihari Vidyabhushan took *sannyasa* initiation from Bhakti Vijnana Ashrama Goswami Maharaja in the presence of many of his *sannyasi* and *brahmachari* godbrothers at Srila Prabhupada's *samadhi mandir*. He got the name Bhakti Vilas Tirtha Goswami Maharaja and eventually became *acharya* of Sri Chaitanya Math and its branches. Srila Bhakti Vilas Tirtha Goswami Maharaja dedicated his time to continuing all of the initiatives that Srila Prabhupada had started and also established various temples like Purushottam Gaudiya Math in Puri, Madanmohan Gaudiya Math in Vrindavan, Chaitanya Research Institute in Calcutta, Gaudiya Math at Diamond Harbor and so on. He also established Rai Ramananda's deity and the lotus footprints of Lord Chaitanya at Kovvur along the banks of the Godavari River. He installed deities and lotus footprints of Sri Chaitanya Mahaprabhu in many parts of India. He also made exhibitions of Lord Chaitanya in various cities such as Calcutta, Dhaka, Patna, Kashi and so on.

On Friday, 10 September 1976 at 3:20 pm, Bhakti Vilas Tirtha Goswami Maharaja physically passed away and left behind his visible transcendental body at Srila Prabhupada's *bhajan kutir* in the presence of many Gaudiya Math *brahmacharis* and *sannyasis*. His entire spiritual life gives us the example of *gurudevatma* – in other words, dedicating one's life completely to the desire of the spiritual master. We know Srila Prabhupada's eternal form is Nayanamani Manjari. Srila Prabhupada revealed Bhakti Vilas Tirtha Goswami Maharaja's spiritual identity as Bimala Manjari.

SRILA BHAKTI VIVEK BHARATI GOSWAMI MAHARAJA

SRILA ANANTA VASUDEV PRABHU

We know that purity is synonymous with becoming popular, which, of course, is not the ultimate goal of a pure devotee (Vaishnava). Srila Ananta Vasudeva Prabhu was one of the disciples of Srila Prabhupada who taught us how to remain aloof from popularity and deeply enter into the eternal transcendental services of the Lord.

Ananta Vasudeva Prabhu was born on 25 August 1895 in the village of Sandeep Hatia located in the district of Noyakhali in present-day Bangladesh. His father was Rajani Kanta Basu,and his mother Srimati Vidhumukhi Devi. Since childhood, Ananta Vasudeva Prabhu had a spontaneous attachment for reading *Srimad Bhagavatam* and chanting devotional songs written by Srila Narottama Das Thakura and by Srila Bhaktivinoda Thakura, while playing the *mridanga* (musical drum made of clay).

On 30 December 1911, along with his father and elder brother (Yogendranath Basu), Ananta Vasudeva Prabhu, who was 16 years old, met Srila Bhaktivinoda Thakura and Bimala Prasad for the first time at the Thakura's residence called Bhakti Bhavan, Rambagan, Calcutta.

In 1918, Ananta Vasudeva Prabhu again met with Srila Prabhupada at Bhakti Bhavan. Once, during his meeting with Srila Prabhupada, Ananta Vasudeva Prabhu melodiously sang, *Kabe Habe Bolo Sei Din Amar*, a song written by Srila Bhaktivinoda Thakura. On the next day, which was the Gaura Purnima festival (appearance day of Lord Sri Chaitanya), he received initiation from Srila Prabhupada and became known as Ananta Vasudeva Prabhu.

In a short period of time, Srila Prabhupada became attracted to his extraordinary devotional charisma and therefore appointed Ananta Vasudeva Prabhu as the chief editor of Bhagavat Press. Ananta Vasudeva Prabhu was known to be extremely intelligent, proficient in Sanskrit and an erudite scholar.

In 1924, Ananta Vasudeva Prabhu was the first personality who inaugurated the glorious worship of Sri Guru termed as Vyasa Puja in the Gaudiya Math, thus giving the devotees an opportunity to observe this auspicious ceremony in honor of the *guru-parampara* (disciplic succession). This allowed the devotees to understand the significance of such an important festival. Furthermore, he conducted the 50th Vyasa Puja festival of Srila Prabhupada.

After Srila Prabhupada departed from this world on 1 January 1937, on 26 March 1937 Ananta Vasudeva Prabhu was unanimously selected by his godbrothers to be the successor *acharya* of the Gaudiya Math. In June 1939, he took the *sannyasa* (renunciation) vow and was ordained with the new name, Srila Bhakti Prasad Puri Das Thakura.

In 1941, Srila Puri Das Thakura felt inspired to change the society's name from Gaudiya Math into Gaudiya Mission.

In 1943, Srila Puri Das Thakura felt that his incredible popularity was becoming a disturbance to his devotional practice. He therefore manifested a 'deception' pastime (which laymen cannot understand). He abandoned the position of the *acharya* in preference to performing solitary spiritual practices, thereby relishing the eternal service of the Divine Couple (Sri Sri Radha-Krishna) in Vrindavan.

In 1954, he appointed his godbrother Srila Bhakti Kevala Audulomi Goswami Maharaja to the *acharya* post of the Gaudiya Mission. Later, he printed almost all of the rare books of the *goswamis* and distributed them freely amongst local schools and libraries.

On 8 March 1958, Srila Puri Das Thakura departed from this mortal world. Throughout his life, by example, he taught us that no one is able to realize a pure devotee's activities using their mundane intelligence.

Srila Prabhupada commented on Ananta Vasudev Prabhu, saying that he is the 'Ganesh' of the Gaudiya Math – because of his role of transcribing the *Bhagavatam*. Just as Srila Vyasa Dev (who is the energy incarnation of Lord Sri Krishna) instructed Ganesh to transcribe the *Bhagavatam*, similarly, Ananta Vasudev Prabhu was the Ganesh of Srila Bhaktisiddhanta Thakura. Whenever Srila Prabhupada would forget a *shloka* (scriptural verse) during *harikatha* (discourse), Ananta Vasudev Prabhu would immediately remind him.

CHAPTER FORTY

SRILA KRISHNADAS BABAJI MAHARAJA

All around the world, everyone is looking for happiness in the various mundane sources without understanding that the true fountainhead of pleasure is the Supreme Lord alone. In this age of quarrel and hypocrisy, the master and controller of ultimate joy has given us a simple and efficient means of achieving spiritual perfection. He has Himself become present in this world in His own names and has set no restrictive rules or regulations for chanting them. His only instruction is to chant these Holy Names always and everywhere. Through the chanting of these Holy Names, all of one's desires will be fulfilled. Krishnadas Babaji's extraordinary life is living proof that all this is true. Although Srila Krishnadas Babaji lived in one tiny corner of the world, his life offers a beacon-like example for all humanity of how everyone can seek out and find happiness in the Divine through taking shelter of the *maha-mantra* (*Hare Krishna Hare Krishna, Krishna Krishna Hare Hare, Hare Rama Hare Rama, Rama Rama Hare Hare*).

Srila Krishnadas Babaji Maharaja was born a little over a century ago in a respectable family in Bikrampur, in the present-day Dhaka district of Bangladesh. He was related to Chittaranjan Das, a famous lawyer and activist for Indian independence and had himself graduated with honors from Dhaka University with a BA degree. He seemed set for an illustrious career in law. However, Krishna Das had a strong thirst for spiritual life. His parents were very pious and embarked on regular pilgrimage to the holy places along the Ganges like Prayag, Benares, Haridwar and Rishikesh. Krishna Das had also visited Haridwar and Rishikesh several times, but each time returned disappointed, for he was seeking a *sat-guru* (bona fide preceptor). He found no solace in the impersonalistic doctrines taught by most holy men in these places.

In 1920, just as he was losing hope of finding a genuine spiritual teacher, Srila Prabhupada visited Dhaka with his preaching party. Krishna Das came to Srila Prabhupada's program, and upon seeing Srila Prabhupada immediately felt that he would be his eternal spiritual master. He spontaneously decided to take initiation from Srila Prabhupada. Srila Prabhupada's discourses were for him like the final arrival of the rains after a long, parching dry season.

A year later, Srila Prabhupada accepted Krishna Das as his disciple and gave him the *brahmachari* name Sadhikananda Das. After initiation, Sadhikananda committed himself fully to the chanting of the Holy Name, following the example of Lord Chaitanya's associate Haridas Thakura. He stayed at the *brahmachari* dormitory in Chaitanya Math in Mayapur, where, in line with Srila Prabhupada's instructions, he chanted the *maha-mantra* nonstop, behind closed doors, all day long.

Sadhikananda was soon put to the test by his own godbrothers. Such is the nature of the age we live in. Some of the other devotees felt that Sadhikananda was neglecting performing the menial tasks around the *math*, usually given to the *brahmacharis*, and thought that his imitation of Haridas Thakura's exalted example was artificial. Sadhikananda was honoring the *math prasad* without contributing to its upkeep. They complained to Srila Prabhupada and were surprised to hear the master defend his disciple. One day, after having heard these complaints again and again, Srila Prabhupada said, "If any of you are able to chant like Sadhikananda, you live in a similar manner, where your needs are met without any obligation. Krishna is the proprietor of all things. Taking complete shelter of His Holy Name means to take full shelter of Him. I want all of you to take shelter of the Lord and His name. If we can do this, then the

Lord Himself will send us more of His servants to take care of the other aspects of temple service."

On hearing Srila Prabhupada's words, some of the complainers tried to imitate Sadhikananda, but none was able to match his natural enthusiasm for chanting. Within a few days, all of them had returned to their habitual service and all their criticisms stopped. Even so, Sadhikananda felt uneasy about staying in the *math* after this incident. Fearing that the master would again be pestered in this manner, one night he quietly paid his obeisances to Srila Prabhupada and set off on foot for Rishikesh, a famous holy place where impersonalist renunciates go to meditate. His intention was to devote himself exclusively to the chanting of the Holy Name and set an example for the *Mayavadis*. His message was: "Give up your idea that worshiping the Lord is imaginary. The Lord has descended as His own Holy Name. So just take shelter of the *maha-mantra* and you will achieve success in your efforts at perfecting spiritual life."

In the meantime, Srila Prabhupada was distressed by Sadhikananda's departure and asked his disciples to do whatever they could to bring him back. Srila Bon Maharaja, an unparalleled orator to whom Srila Prabhupada first confided the task of preaching Lord Chaitanya's message in the West, went to Hardwar and told Sadhikananda that Srila Prabhupada wanted him to come back to Sri Mayapur. Sadhikananda could not disobey his *gurudeva* and returned to Mayapur with Bon Maharaja.

On his return, Srila Prabhupada gave Sadhikananda a separate room and told him clearly that his only duty was to chant the Hare Krishna *maha-mantra*. With Srila Prabhupada's blessings, Sadhikananda would chant the Holy Names in *kirtan* for eight hours every day and then on his beads for the remaining sixteen. A few devotees did not believe that he was really chanting for all twenty-four hours of every day and decided to investigate; but were astonished to find that it was indeed true. Others again tried to imitate his lifestyle but were still unable to do so. No one could understand how Sadhikananda could chant for twenty-four hours a day. However, by the mercy of the spiritual master all things are made possible – the dumb become eloquent and the lame climb mountains. After reciting the *Srimad Bhagavatam* for a full seven days, Srila Sukadeva Goswami asked Parikshit Maharaja whether he was hungry or tired. Parikshit replied, "The *Srimad Bhagavatam* is the wish-fulfilling tree of the *Vedas*, the essence of all *Upanishads*. Hearing it gives me the sweetest taste of fruit nectar, *rasamalai*. By your grace, I have been drinking this *rasamalai* over the past seven days, so I am not feeling hungry at all." The nectar of the Holy Name is such that when one gets a taste for it, one forgets even food and sleep.

The criticism that Sadhikananda received from his godbrothers was actually a blessing in disguise as it drew attention to him and made him dearer to his *gurudeva*, attracting special mercy. Through his constant chanting of the Holy Name, Babaji Maharaja was later able to realize his original form as a cowherd companion of the Lord, associating with Him eternally in His abode, Goloka.

The above account shows that the Vaishnava's curse or criticism is never what it seems, but actually a blessing. A similar example is evident in the pastime of Nalakuvera and Manigriva, who were both cursed by Narada Muni to become trees. This curse ultimately led to them both being freed by Lord Krishna Himself, during His *damodar-lila*. Their curse was actually the blessing that afforded them the opportunity to receive Sri Krishna's *darshan*.

Sadhikananda Brahmachari thus had no interest in eating fine prasadam or wearing opulent clothes. He used to wear a very short *dhoti*. He lived according to Mahaprabhu's instruction to Raghunath Das Goswami: *bhālo nā khāibe, bhālo nā paribe*, which means to not eat or dress well. After initiation, instead of seeking material comforts, he chanted very carefully, like Haridas Thakura, teaching us all that chanting the Holy Name is the essence of human life in *Kali-yuga*.

Approximately two or three months before Srila Prabhupada's physical departure from this world, Sadhikananda had a very significant dream. He saw a great procession of devotees led by an elephant and followed by thousands of golden chariots, winding from Calcutta to Mayapur. Heading this procession was Ananta Vasudeva Prabhu, who sat on the elephant. Ananta Vasudeva was a learned scholar, known as Srila Prabhupada's right-hand man. In the dream, Ananta Vasudeva was being followed by the rest of his godbrothers on the golden chariots. Everyone was engaged in an ecstatic *kirtan*. Before they passed through the Sri Chaitanya Math's gate, however, the elephant went mad and picked up Ananta Vasudeva with its trunk, threw him onto the ground, and crushed him under its feet. Panic spread through the other devotees, and the joyful chanting was completely disrupted. Sadhikananda saw the same dream for two days at different times. This dream was narrated to me by Sripad Hariprasad Das Babaji of Nandagram, a disciple of Bhakti Vilasa Tirtha Maharaja, who was Babaji Maharaja's personal assistant and served him over the last few months of his life.

Sadhikananda recognized that the dream was warning him of what was to take place in the Gaudiya Math after Srila Prabhupada's departure. While he was wondering what he would do in that eventuality, Srila

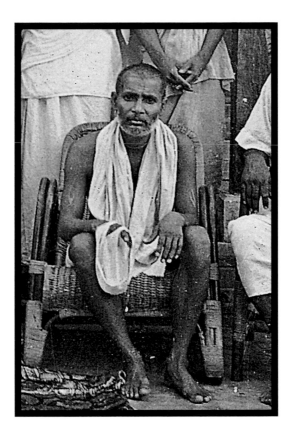

Prabhupada did indeed enter the eternal pastimes of Radha and Govinda on the morning of 1 January 1937. All the clocks in the Bagh Bazaar Gaudiya Math in Calcutta miraculously stopped at 5:30, marking the exact moment of Srila Prabhupada's divine departure. In the turmoil following Srila Prabhupada's entry into *maha samadhi*, Sadhikananda kept aloof from all the politics and refused to join any of the various factions. He left Sri Chaitanya Math and began to wander throughout India, visiting many holy places and living on *madhukari*. For much of this time he was accompanied by my *gurudeva*,

Srila Bhakti Pramode Puri Maharaja. The two friends would joyfully engage in *harinama-sankirtan* on their travels.

Finally, Sadhikananda Das decided to settle in Vrindavan to continue the service of constant chanting given him by Srila Prabhupada. He chose Davanala Kund in Vrindavan to be his place of *bhajan*. He found a cave near the *kund* (pond) for living and chanting, like Haridas Thakura did when he resided near Shantipur in a cave inhabited by a poisonous snake. By living in this way, Haridas Thakura showed us that the Holy Name is our ultimate protector. Similarly, our Srila Sadhikananda Brahmachari gave us the same example by living in a cave near Davanala Kund for six years. While there, he used to take prasad from the nearby *math* of one of his godbrothers, Jachak Maharaja. He then moved to Nanda Maharaja's garden (Nanda Bagicha), halfway between Ter Kadamba and Nandagram, where he stayed for the next six years, continuing to follow the same lifestyle. After that, he established himself at Sanatan Goswami's *bhajan kutir* near Pavan Sarovar. This became his permanent base for the rest of his life, even though he frequently traveled to the various different holy places of Vraja and Gaura Mandals.

After many years of full commitment to the Holy Name, Sadhikananda one day had a dream in which Vamsi Das Babaji Maharaja ordered him to take the dress of a renunciate (*babaji*). He followed this order and accepted the *babaji* dress at Sanatan Goswami's *bhajan kutir* at Nandagram in front of a picture of Srila Prabhupada. After taking the renounced order of life, Sadhikananda adopted the name Krishna Das, "servant of Krishna." By the grace of the Holy Name, he became well known throughout the whole of Vraja by this name. Even after taking the *babaji* order, he hardly spoke to anyone except for uttering the Holy Name. As a result, many of the villagers called him Mauni (silent) Baba.

Krishnadas Babaji Maharaja came to know of his original form as a friend of Krishna through the chanting of Holy Name. It happened in the following way: On one of his parikramas around Vraja Mandala, Krishna Das stopped at the Dauji temple near Gokul. Just like Madhavendra Puri in Remuna, Babaji Maharaja sat down to chant and was dozing off when he suddenly woke with a start and began loudly shouting, "Please take me with you! Please take me with you!" He then fell, senseless. The *brahmana* servants of Dauji saw Babaji Maharaja lying unconscious and took proper care of him, bringing him back to his senses. When they asked him what had happened, he gave no answer. Later, however, he told some close friends what had transpired. He had seen Krishna and Balaram appear from the temple and head for the pasture with a herd of cows. But as they were leaving him behind, Krishna Das had started shouting to them to wait for him. After this incident, Babaji Maharaja always thought of himself as Krishna's cowherd friend and preferred to sing *kirtans* connected to the mood of friendship (*sakhya*). Not only that, but he also cultivated a mood of friendship with all of his godbrothers.

In keeping with this mood of friendship, Babaji Maharaja always moved between the two holy *dhamas*, Vrindavan and Navadwip, the hidden Vrindavan in Bengal. He would spend six months of the year, from January to June, at different *maths* in Bengal. He mostly stayed at Sri Chaitanya Math, which had been established by his *gurudeva,* and in other *maths* established by his godbrothers, such as Sri Chaitanya Gaudiya Math of His Divine Grace Srila Bhakti Dayita Madhava Goswami Maharaja, Sri Chaitanya Saraswata Math of His Divine Grace Srila Bhakti Rakshak Sridhar Dev Goswami

Maharaja, Sri Devananda Gaudiya Math of Srila Bhakti Prajnan Keshava Goswami Maharaja, the Gaura Nityananda temple established by Bhakti Saranga Goswami Maharaja, and Sri Bhajan Ashram of His Divine Grace Srila Bhakti Hridaya Bon Maharaja.

He would spend the remaining six months of the year in the different places in Vraja Mandala mentioned above. While staying in the various *maths* of his godbrothers, Srila Babaji Maharaja would serve the Vaishnavas by leading the *kirtans* and playing the *mridanga*. The rest of time, he would chant the Holy Name on his beads. Through this service and his perennially jolly mood, Babaji Maharaja kept on friendly terms with all of his godbrothers. He had no enemy in the entire Vaishnava community. Everyone eagerly accepted his services and felt extremely fortunate whenever he came to stay in their *math*, even if it was just for a short while.

Krishnadas Babaji Maharaja frequently travelled with his godbrothers when they called on him. In those days, my *gurudeva*, His Divine Grace Srila Bhakti Pramode Puri Goswami Maharaja, had no *math* or society of his own, so on occasion Srila Babaji Maharaja liked to go on pilgrimage with him, all the while maintaining his own *bhajan* practice. On one such pilgrimage, he accompanied my *gurudeva* and another godbrother, Srila Ratha Prabhu (later known as Srila Bhakti Kamal Abadhut Maharaja), to Ayodhya, the land of Lord Ramachandra.

One day, Ratha Prabhu got very hungry and purchased a few guavas in the market for the three of them to eat. There were many Ramanandi *sadhus* (sages) in the same place, each of whom had his own *kamandalu* (a metal water pot with a spout). Unaware that the Ramanandi *sadhus* prohibited anyone else from touching their water pots, Ratha Prabhu quite innocently took one of them to wash his guavas, without first asking for permission. As soon as he touched the *kamandalu*, however, its owner rushed up to him, snatched it and began to rebuke him in the most impolite language. The other assembled Ramanandi *sadhus* surrounded Ratha Prabhu and threatened to beat him up for his action. However, Srila Gurudeva and Srila Babaji Maharaja's asked the *sadhus* why they were so angry. The Ramanandi *sadhu* answered, "If you fish-eating Bengalis touch my pot, it becomes contaminated and that will ruin my spiritual practice." My *gurudeva* said, "You are mistaken. This man is our godbrother and a saintly man who strictly follows a vegetarian diet. No harmful effects will come from his touching your water pot." Some of the Ramanandis said, "Maybe he doesn't eat fish, but his father surely did." Guru Maharaja and Babaji Maharaja began to quote from various scriptures to prove that such an understanding was completely false, but they did it in such a humble and polite way that the Ramanandis calmed down and forgot their complaint. The spiritual strength of Srila Prabhupada's three disciples and the scriptural arguments of Srila Puri Maharaja defused the situation and the Ramanandis left them alone.

This incident reminds us of how Sriman Mahaprabhu converted the Kazi and the victory of Srila Haridas Thakura over his oppressors. Once Srila Haridas Thakura was beaten by the soldiers of the local Muslim magistrate (the Kazi) in 21 public squares because Haridas would not comply with his order to stop chanting the Holy Name. The grace of the Lord's Holy Name protected Srila Haridas Thakura from suffering any phsyical harm from this cruel punishment. In another incident, the *Kazi* of Navadwip broke the *mridanga* (drum) used in *kirtan* at Srivas Pandit's house and prohibited the public chanting of the Holy Name. Mahaprabhu challenged him by organising all His devotees in a large *sankirtan* party, leading them to the Kazi's house to protest the ban. The *Kazi* finally surrendered to Mahaprabhu's lotus feet and became a full-fledged devotee. Similarly, Babaji Maharaja's pure devotional attitude had a transformative power over negative energies like anger.

By the grace of Srila Prabhupada and the Holy Name, Srila Babaji Maharaja was totally free from any kind of mundane attachment. He once bought a piece of land in Raman Reti in Vrindavan in order to establish his own preaching center or *math* for the benefit of conditioned individuals like ourselves. He had received some financial backing from a householder devotee and began to buy building materials like bricks and sand, which were meant for a wall and a small building. When Babaji Maharaja went to his plot with a surveyor, however, he saw that the owner of the neighboring property had encroached on his land, appropriating about a foot of it from one side. When Babaji Maharaja confronted his neighbor, the neighbor did not agree to give up even an inch of the land he had taken. Babaji Maharaja was saddened to see such mundane aggressiveness and realized that the desire to own property was at the root of so many problems in life, especially if one wants to engage in *bhajan*. He immediately told the person, "My land and whatever materials are stored here are yours. I don't want to get involved in mundane quarrels. Please take it all and do whatever you like with it." The greedy neighbor was astonished and ashamed to receive the magnanimity of Babaji Maharaja. With this action Babaji Maharaja demonstrated the futility of fighting for acquisitions like land and buildings. The real value in our short lifespan comes from engaging in Hari *bhajan*.

Krishnadas Babaji Maharaja never swerved from Srila Prabhupada's instruction to live simply and give full commitment to hearing, chanting and meditating on Lord Krishna. At the same time, however, he also contributed to *gurudeva*'s preaching mission. I heard the following story from Sri Banwarilal Singhania, a businessman devotee based in Calcutta. Banwarilal and his entire family were very much drawn to Babaji Maharaja's perfect Vaishnava humility and desired to render some service to his lotus feet. Babaji Maharaja repeatedly refused to take any form of service from them in accordance with his lifelong vow. Nevertheless, when Banwarilal approached him one day in his *bhajan kutir* at Pavan Sarovar and asked him once again how he could serve him, Babaji Maharaja replied that he would certainly engage him in his most worshipable *gurudeva*'s service when inspired by his *gurudeva*. This opportunity arose shortly thereafter.

Babaji Maharaja happened to be visiting Calcutta on a day of a total solar eclipse. He was staying at a *grihastha* Vaishnava's temple and had committed himself to performing *kirtan* throughout the duration of the solar eclipse as is recommended in the Gaudiya Vaishnava tradition. Banwarilal heard about this and went to the temple with two friends to join Srila Babaji Maharaja in the *kirtan*. When the eclipse and the exhilarating *kirtan* came to an end, Srila Babaji Maharaja went to take a shower, chanting prayers to the lotus feet of his *gurudeva* composed by Srila B. R. Sridhar Maharaja (*sujanarbudaradhita-pada-yugam*). When he returned, he stood before Banwarilal and his friends with folded hands and said, "According to Vedic tradition, it is very auspicious to give in charity to a poor *brahmana*. Although I am not a *brahmana*..." Before he could finish his sentence, Banwarilal got up, very excited and full of anticipation. He asked what he, an ordinary businessman, could possibly give in charity to a great devotee like Srila Babaji Maharaja. Maharaja humbly replied that whereas all his godbrothers had over the years rendered valuable service to his worshipful spiritual master and his transcendental preaching mission, he himself had spent his days as a parasite, simply eating and sleeping at the expense of his *gurudeva*'s mission. On this day, however, he had been inspired by his spiritual master to be instrumental in whatever way he could to assist his godbrother Srila Bhakti Dayita Madhava Goswami Maharaja in recovering the birth site of his spiritual master on the Grand Road in Jagannath Puri and building a monument there. Banwarilal was so overwhelmed by Srila Babaji Maharaja's humility and the wonderful opportunity to serve an eternal associate of the Supreme Lord that he immediately fell down at Babaji Maharaja's lotus feet. He committed himself to becoming one of the most important contributors to the construction of the temple and *sankirtan* hall on the site. The cornerstone was laid on 24 March 1980 and a beautiful skyscraping temple, which houses Sriman Mahaprabhu and Jagannath Deva, was officially consecrated on 5 February 1982, the holy advent anniversary of Srila Prabhupada. To this day Banwarilal is ever grateful to Srila Babaji Maharaja for having engaged him in this transcendental service. It may be said that we Gaudiya Vaishnavas, spiritual descendants of Srila Prabhupada, are able to offer our respect and obeisances to his lotus feet on the site of his birth through the direct mercy of Srila Krishnadas Babaji Maharaja.

Towards the end worldly lifespan, Babaji Maharaja manifested the pastime of appearing to be ill and was thus taken by his well-wishers to the Agra Hospital. When the doctor examined him with his stethoscope, he was astonished to hear the Holy Name vibrating in the stethoscope instead of the sounds of Babaji Maharaja's heartbeat as expected. All he heard was the sound of the *maha-mantra* (*Hare Krishna Hare Krishna, Krishna Krishna Hare Hare, Hare Rama Hare Rama, Rama Rama Hare Hare*). The doctor was puzzled and examined him again, with the same results. He then called his associates to also examine Babaji Maharaja, but everyone heard the same holy sound emanating from his chest. Unable to find any illness, they released Babaji Maharaja and he returned to Pavan Sarovar.

Through this and other pastimes Srila Babaji Maharaja personified Srila Bhaktivinoda Thakura's teachings as found in his *kirtan, Jiva Jago*:

> *jīvana anitya jānaha sār,*
> *tāhe nānā-vidha vipada-bhār,*
> *nāmāśraya kori' jatane tumi,*
> *thākaha āpana kāje*

"Life is temporary and full of so many dangers. The body will be destroyed either today or tomorrow, so don't waste your time just doing your mundane work. We have to do our eternal job in order to reach the ultimate goal of life. Chanting the Holy Name alone is eternal in the universe. So please take shelter of the Holy Name and engage peacefully in service connected to the Holy Name."

In the *Chaitanya Bhagavat*, it is said that whatever seems to be distress in a Vaishnava's life is in fact the greatest joy.

> *yata dekha vaiṣṇavera vyavahāra duḥkha*
> *niścaya jāniha tāhā paramānanda-sukha*

I once saw Babaji Maharaja and Bhakti Srirupa Siddhanti Maharaja get into an argument. Though it looked pretty serious, it was only a friendly quarrel. Although Babaji Maharaja chanted three lakhs of Holy Names every day, when in Navadwip he sometimes went to listen to the *lila kirtans* enacted by the Sahajiyas. Siddhanti Maharaja teased him, saying, "O three-lakhs-a-day Babaji Mahashay! You don't get enough *Krishna lila* from chanting three lakhs of Krishna's names? You need to go listen to the Sahajiyas' *kirtan*? Why are you making a mockery of Srila Prabhupada's standards?"

Babaji Maharaja said nothing in response to his godbrother's criticisms but returned immediately to Sanatan Goswami's *bhajan kutir*, where he started to fast. Bon Maharaja, Sridhar Maharaja and many other godbrothers wrote him letters and sent messengers asking him to stop his fast and to return to his normal life. However, it was all to no avail. The Supreme Lord decided to withdraw him from our mortal vision and take him to His own bosom. On Monday, 12 April 1982, at 09:00, Srila Krishnadas Babaji Maharaja entered into the Lord's cow-herding pastimes, casting us all into an ocean of bereavement.

Many devotees still make the trip to Pavan Sarovar just to see Krishnadas Babaji Maharaja's *samadhi* temple, which is being taken care of by some members of the Gaudiya Math in the renounced order. We also pray for his blessings: May he grant us love for the Holy Name and affection for the association of Vaishnavas.

CHAPTER FORTY-ONE

SRILA MADANMOHAN DAS ADHIKARI

On 19 March 1914 (Bengali calendar: 5 Caitra 1320), a spiritually special baby boy was born in Kanpur village, Howrah District, West Bengal. His parents, Purnachandra Seth and Kadambini Devi, named the baby Madanamohana Seth. From a very early age, Madanamohana was spiritually inclined but did not receive proper spiritual guidance from his family members. Under family duress, he married at the age of 14 to Parulbala Devi, who was nine years old at the time. Although he did not have a formal education, Madanamohana was proficient in reading and writing in Bengali. When he was 23 years old, his first child, a daughter, Reba, was born.

Madanamohana often frequented Calcutta to buy goods for his business, which was situated in Polerhat/ Mograhat, South 24-Parganas, West Bengal. One day in July 1936, Madanamohana Seth was near the banks of the Ganges in Calcutta and was contemplating taking bath in the holy river. He noticed an attractive festival going on in a beautiful temple (it was the Bag Bazar Gaudiya Math). He entered the temple campus and after paying obeisance to the deities of Sri Sri Radha-Krishna, he met Srila Sagar Maharaja, a *sannyasi* disciple of Srila Prabhupada. The entire temple atmosphere was so attractive that he felt that he was in the right place for practicing spirituality. Srila Sagar Maharaja inspired Madanamohana to wait and listen to Srila Prabhupada's spiritual discourses.

As soon as the youthful Madanamohana, 23 years of age, saw Srila Prabhupada, he was inexplicably drawn to Srila Prabhupada. Hearing *harikatha* (spiritual discourse) from Srila Prabhupada, he was captivated and his outlook on life changed completely. Madanamohana had just stepped into the temple to visit the festival for a few hours but ended up staying for three days at the Gaudiya Math just to listen to Srila Prabhupada's discourses. On the third day, Srila Prabhupada was giving initiations to some devotees. Srila Sagar Maharaja inspired Madanamohana to take initiation from Srila Prabhupada. Srila Prabhupada's room was full of devotees who were aspiring to take initiation, many of whom were rejected. Madanamohana Seth was among the few that were accepted. Srila Prabhupada gave Madanamohana *harinama* (first initiation), and he was known from then onwards as Madanamohana Das Adhikari Prabhu.

Approximately five months later, Srila Prabhupada physically passed away from this material world on 1 January 1937. According to the instruction of his *gurudeva*, Madanamohana Prabhu wholeheartedly served all of his godbrothers and Srila Prabhupada's mission physically, financially and mentally. Over time, Madanamohana Prabhu became the father of eight daughters and three sons, and the grandfather of 26 grandchildren, one of whom is me. Every single one of Madanamohana Prabhu's children and grandchildren became devotees of the Gaudiya Math and was duly initiated.

Madanamohana Prabhu respected all of his godbrothers and saw them as being non-different from his *gurudeva*. He always said that all of his godbrothers were liberated personalities (*jivana-mukta-purusa*). Therefore, he took all of his grandchildren to all of his godbrothers without discrimination and his children chose their spiritual masters accordingly. Whenever any Vaishnava came to his village home, he used to serve them as if the Supreme Lord had come, understanding that all Vaishnavas are the Supreme Lord's representatives.

His Divine Grace Srila Bhakti Pramode Puri Goswami Thakura used to come to Madanamohana Prabhu's village home every year. In order to spread the glories of his *gurudeva*'s mission, Madanamohana Prabhu

used to arrange *pandal* (marquee) programs and home programs throughout the village wherein the visiting Vaishnava would give discourses. These discourses were broadcasted across the village using loudspeakers. Throughout his life, he exemplified how a real devotional householder should be. In his last years, Madanamohana Prabhu's thoughts and actions were infused with his *gurudeva*. If it didn't rain, he would say, "This is the desire of Prabhupada." If there was loss in the business, he would say, "This is the desire of Prabhupada." He saw everything happening as the desire of his *gurudeva*. Even when Madanamohana Prabhu got a heart problem a few days before his physical departure, he said that it was the desire of Srila Prabhupada.

At 22:10 on Monday, 3 April 2006 (Bengali Calendar: 20 Caitra 1412), a dark period dawned upon the whole Vaishnava community as one of the few remaining disciples of Srila Prabhupada, Madanamohana Prabhu, departed from this world while uttering the name of his *gurudeva*, "Jaya Prabhupada. Jaya Prabhupada." Madanamohana Prabhu's entire life represents the principle of *guru-nistha*, having unshakably firm faith on one's spiritual master.

CHAPTER FORTY-TWO

SRILA NAYANANANDA DAS BABAJI MAHARAJA

The Supreme Personality of Godhead's pleasure potency is Srimati Radha Thakurani. In order to distribute the bliss of Srimati Radharani, Sri Sacinandana was born as the son of Sri Govardhana Dutta and Srimati Sarada Devi in the village of Jahanabad, Khejuri, Midnapore, West Bengal. In the year 1928, at the age of 21, Sacinandana joined the mission of his *gurudeva*, Srila Prabhupada, on the auspicious day of Gaura Purnima at Sri Chaitanya Math located in Sridhama Mayapur.

He served Sri Chaitanya Math wholeheartedly under the shelter of Sri Vinode Bihari (later known as Srila Bhakti Prajnan Keshava Goswami). After three years, in 1931, upon seeing his service attitude and mood for following in the footsteps of Srila Keshava Goswami Maharaja and all the senior Vaishnavas, Srila Prabhupada happily gave him *harinama* and *diksha* (first and second initiation). After initiation, his name became Satprasangananda Das Brahmachari, and all the devotees used to call him Satish Prabhu.

After initiation, Srila Prabhupada appointed him to serve the deities of Gaura Gadadhar at Champahatti. These deities were installed by Dwija Vaninatha, the brother of Gadadhar Pandit. Champahatti is located in the island of Ritudvipa (one of the nine islands of Navadwip) and represents Khadirvana, one of the 12 forests of Vrindavan.

For 69 years (1931 to 2000), Satprasangananda Das Brahmachari (Satish Prabhu) wholeheartedly followed the order of Srila Prabhupada. In 1990, at Sri Gopinath Gaudiya Math in Mayapur on Srila Prabhupada's Vyasapuja day, he took *babaji* initiation from his godbrother His Divine Grace Srila Bhakti Pramode Puri Goswami Thakura and received the name Srila Nayanananda Das Babaji Maharaja.

Due to his old age and the antagonistic mood of some *brahmacharis*, he was forced to leave his service at Champahatti and subsequently stayed at Sri Gopinath Gaudiya Math, Ishodyan, Mayapur. After Srila Bhakti Pramode Puri Goswami Thakura's physical departure, through a unanimous vote, Srila Nayanananda Das Babaji became the president of the World Vaishnava Association.

On 21 January 2003, in the early hours of the morning after the *mangala arati* at Sri Gopinath Gaudiya Math, he physically left this world. He was put into *samadhi* on the same day on the temple premises at Sri Gopinath Gaudiya Math, Mayapur. He left his spirit, service attitude and teachings behind for all of us. If one follows his exemplary devotional teachings, that person can get pure devotion and be delivered from this miserable world. Srila Nayananda Das Babaji's last surviving disciple, Sri Sajjan Das Brahmachari, currently serves at Sri Gopinath Gaudiya Math, Ishodyan, Mayapur.

CHAPTER FORTY-THREE

SRILA PURUSHOTTAM DAS BRAHMACHARI

Srila Purushottam Das Brahmachari was born on Sunday, 17 October 1915 in a wealthy devotee's family. It was the day of Vijaya Dasami (10ᵗʰ day of the waxing moon, Keshava), when Lord Ramachandra conquered Ravana in Lanka. At the age of 19, he started to travel around India and reached Sri Ramananda Gaudiya Math, located on the western bank of the Godavari River in Kovvur, Andhra Pradesh. He enjoyed attending the daily temple programs.

On 1 April 1934, he began staying at Sri Ramananda Gaudiya Math. After seven days, on Sunday, 8 April, Srila Prabhupada arrived at Sri Ramananda Gaudiya Math and saw two new inquisitive devotees, later known as Raghava Chaitanya Das Brahmachari and Purushottam Das Brahmachari.

On Tuesday, 26 February 1935 (eighth day of the waning moon in the *Vedic* month of Phalguna) Srila Prabhupada gave him *diksha* (second initiation) and the name Sri Purushottam Das Brahmachari at Purushottam Math located in Jagannath Puri Dhama. Purushottam Prabhu was extremely austere, similar to Raghunath Das Goswami. Purushottam Prabhu and Raghava Chaitanya Prabhu became close friends and enthusiastically preached the loving message of Lord Chaitanya under the shelter of their *gurudeva*, Srila Prabhupada.

After Srila Prabhupada's physical departure in 1937, Purushottam Prabhu used to preach along with Raghava Chaitanya Das Brahmachari around India. They eventually decided to permanently reside in Vrindavan (*akhanda-vrindavan-vas*) and publish rare books of the *goswami*s. In 1967, after Raghav Chaitanya Prabhu's physical departure, Purushottam Prabhu felt lonely and often used to cry with the expression, "Krishna mercifully gave me the association of his devotee but unfortunately, I have now lost the association (*krsna more krpa kari' diyachilena sanga, durbhagyera phale aja mora haila sanga bhanga*).

By nature, Srila Purushottam Prabhu did not like to take donations from anyone except for some selected devotees.

In 1983, Purushottam Prabhu met one of his godbrothers, Madanamohana Das Adhikari (Madanmohan Seth), my maternal grandfather, and inspired him to buy the residence where he used to stay. Madanamohana Prabhu, according to the order of his godbrother Purushottam Prabhu, purchased the residence and happily received his association. On 27 November 1994 (10th day of the waxing moon in the month of Agrahayana, a day before Utpanna Ekadasi), Purushottam Das Brahmachari departed from this material world at 2:45 AM at 117 Gopinath Gehra.

Before his physical departure, he exhibited a transcendental pastime as follows. Fifteen days prior to his physical departure, his voice was choked up and his eyes were always closed due to a cerebral stroke. However, an hour before his departure, his eyes opened, and with a smiling face, he eagerly looked towards the ceiling. At the time, he was surrounded by Prabha Devi Dasi, Tamal Krishna Das, and a few family members of Madanamohana Das Adhikari. They repeatedly asked him, "Uncle, what are you looking at on the ceiling?" He replied, "Krishna with the cowherd boys." He was enjoying that scene for almost five minutes. Then, he again closed his eyes. After about 10 to 15 minutes, he opened his eyes again, looking at the ceiling in a similar manner with a smiling face. All the surrounding members again asked, "Uncle, what are you looking at on the ceiling?" Purushottam Prabhu replied, "Radharani with her *sakhis* (associates)." After five minutes, he again closed his eyes. After 10 to 15 minutes, he again opened his eyes and with a smiling face eagerly looked at the ceiling and chanted, "Srila Prabhupada". All of the surrounding devotees were asking, "Uncle, what are you looking at on the ceiling?" He repeatedly said, "Srila Prabhupada. Srila Prabhupada. Srila Prabhupada". In this manner, he left the material world.

CHAPTER FORTY-FOUR

SRILA RAGHAV CHAITANYA DAS BRAHMACHARI

On Saturday, 28 July 1905 (the 12th day of the waning moon in the Vedic month of Sravana), Sri Raghav Chaitanya Das was born in a landowner's family in the state of Kerala located in southern India. After his birth, his parents and grandparents consulted an astrologer who predicted that the child would not stay at home and would instead take up the renounced order of life. His family arranged for a bodyguard to constantly stay with him so that he would not be able to leave from home.

As per the prediction, the child was always seeking out the association of *sadhus*, but his family kept preventing this from happening. One day, his grandparents requested him to go to the post office to send a letter. He posted the letter as instructed, but also did not want to lose the opportunity. So, he left from the post office on a journey around India to find the association of *sadhus* and to take shelter of a *guru*.

On Sunday, 1 April 1934, he arrived at Sri Ramananda Gaudiya Math, located on the western bank of the Godavari River at Kovvur, Andhra Pradesh. There, he enjoyed the association of *sadhus* and Vaishnavas at the temple, attended *mangala arati* and listened to discourses twice or thrice a day. All the devotees residing in the temple appreciated his behavior. Fortunately, after one week, Srila Prabhupada arrived at the Math. The next day Srila Prabhupada gave him *harinama* (first) initiation.

After 10 months, on Tuesday, 26 February 1935 (the eighth day of the waning-moon cycle in the Vedic month of Phalguna), Srila Prabhupada gave him *diksha* (second) initiation at Purushottam Math, located in Jagannath Puri Dhama. He received the name Sri Raghav Chaitanya Das Brahmachari. After initiation, Srila Prabhupada gave him the service to spread the loving mission of Lord Chaitanya around India.

Raghav Chaitanya Prabhu was fluent in 12 languages and used to preach in Gujarat, Kerala, Tamil Nadu, and Andhra Pradesh. Srila Prabhupada was pleased seeing his skills in preaching. After Srila Prabhupada's physical departure from this world, in order to continue his service Raghav Chaitanya Prabhu preached around India and became an initiating *guru*. Eventually, he decided that he would permanently reside in Vrindavan (*akhanda-vrindavan-vas*). While in Vrindavan, with the help of one of his godbrothers, Srila Purushottam Das Brahmachari Prabhu, he published many rare books of the *goswamis* along with his own commentaries (e.g. *Padyavali, Bhakti-grantha-mala, Krsnananda-mahakavya,* Jiva Goswami's *Gopala Champu* and so on). Sri Raghav Chaitanya Das Brahmachari Prabhu was a hidden treasure. On 23 August 1967, he departed from this world at 7:40 AM from 117 Gopinath Gehra, situated beside Srila Madhu Pandit's *samadhi* in Vrindavan.

CHAPTER FORTY-FIVE

SRILA SAKHI CHARAN DAS BABAJI MAHARAJA

Srila Prabhupada had a magnetic personality that attracted everybody, even those engrossed in business. Sri Sakhi Charan Ray (later known as Srila Sakhi Charan Das Babaji) was one such businessman who became very much attracted to Srila Prabhupada.

Sakhi Charan Ray was born in present-day Bangladesh in the Kashiyani village, Faridpur District in the year 1881 (Bengali year 1288). During that time, Faridpur was located in India. He came to Calcutta seeking to engage in business, and eventually expanded his business into the town of Navadwip. In the year 1915, Sakhi Charan Ray met his *gurudeva*, Sri Bimala Prasad. At the time, Bimala Prasad was amidst his vow to chant one billion holy names. Bimala Prasad's pure character and powerful discourses on the *Bhagavatam* attracted Sakhi Charan Ray towards the Vaishnava lineage. He understood that without taking shelter of a pure Vaishnava, it would not be possible to deliver himself from this miserable world and to achieve eternal peace and bliss. He also realized that his business and wealth were not the keys to getting an eternally peaceful and blissful life. Eventually, Sakhi Charan Ray left his business and took shelter of his *gurudeva*, receiving *harinama* and *diksha* (first and second initiation) on the same day.

Thereafter, Sakhi Charan Ray maintained his life in accordance with the direction of his *gurudeva*, which was to simultaneously maintain his business in India, which was called Sakhi Charan Ray and Sons Pvt. Ltd, alongside serving Krishna. Seeing his service attitude for Mahaprabhu's mission, Srila Prabhupada, gave him the title 'Bhakti Vijay' (one who has conquered devotion).

Bhaktivinoda Thakura had a vision wherein he saw that a most wonderful temple (*adbhuta-mandira*) would appear at Lord Chaitanya's birthplace. Furthermore, at Chaitanya Math, Srila Prabhupada used to stay at Bhakti

Vijay Bhavan, which was his *bhajan kutir*. Both the temple at Lord Chaitanya's birthplace (*adbhuta-mandira*) and Srila Prabhupada's *bhajan kutir* at Chaitanya Math (Bhakti Vijay Bhavan) were sponsored by Sakhi Charan Ray. He also sponsored to print many books, like *Chaitanya Charitamrta*, *Chaitanya Bhagavat* and other publications. In order to fulfill Srila Prabhupada's desire to spread the loving mission of Lord Chaitanya in the western world, Sakhi Charan Ray gave financial support to Bhakti Saranga Goswami Maharaja, Bhakti Pradip Tirtha Goswami Maharaja and Bhakti Hridaya Bon Goswami Maharaja when they went to the western countries to preach. In this way, he used to assist in expanding Srila Prabhupada's and Mahaprabhu's mission.

On Friday, 25 August 1953 (9 Bhadra 1360) on Baladeva's appearance day, Sakhi Charan Ray took *babaji vesh* from Bhakti Saranga Goswami Maharaja and was given name Srimad Sakhi Charan Das Babaji Maharaja. For about eight to nine years, he did intense chanting of the holy names and meditation on Sri Sri Radha Krishna at Bhakti Saranga Goswami's temple located at Imli-tala, Vrindavan. On 1 November 1961 (15th day of Kartik 1368), he disappeared from this world. Srila Sakhi Charan Das Babaji Maharaja's service attitude towards his *gurudeva* inspires all of us to dedicate our very existence to the service of Sri Guru, Vaishnavas and Bhagavan.

CONCLUSION

Maharaja Bhagiratha had, many thousands of years ago, brought the Ganges River down from the heavenly realm to this mundane world to deliver his ancestors. Since that time, the river Ganges has been purifying the souls of this world. Similarly, through the call of His Divine Grace (HDG) Srila Saccidananda Bhaktivinoda Thakura, HDG Srila Prabhupada Bhaktisiddhanta Saraswati Goswami Thakura, who is Radharani's Nayanamani Manjari, descended from the eternal spiritual world into this material world, along with his eternally perfect associates, in order to fulfill the desire of Lord Chaitanya. His preaching, teachings and influence continue to deliver the fallen souls in this age of darkness and hypocrisy, even after his physical departure.

HDG Srila Prabhupada Bhaktisiddhanta Saraswati Thakura's disciples, grand-disciples, great-grand-disciples and great-great-grand-disciples are expanding Lord Chaitanya Mahaprabhu's mission established under various names, such as Sri Chaitanya Gaudiya Math (founder *acharya*: HDG Srila Bhakti Dayita Madhava Goswami Maharaja), Sri Chaitanya Saraswat Math (founder *acharya:* HDG Srila Sridhar Goswami Maharaja), Sri Gopinath Gaudiya Math (founder *acharya*: Srila Bhakti Pramode Puri Goswami Thakura), International Society for Krishna Consciousness (ISKCON) (founder acharya: HDG Srila Bhaktivedanta Swami Prabhupada), and so on. All are branches of the Gaudiya Math established by Srila Prabhupada. Srila Prabhupada's and Srila Bhaktivinoda Thakura's teachings are to establish spontaneous love in the hearts of people, the type of love that the *gopis*, who always follow in the footsteps of

Srimati Radharani and always render service to Krishna, have.

Whoever keeps such goals and propagates the message of Lord Chaitanya, following in the footsteps of our previous teachers (*guru-varga*), are all considered to be followers of Gaudiya *math* or mission. Whoever wholeheartedly executes all the instructions of our *guru-varga*, Srila Prabhupada Bhaktisiddhanta Saraswati Goswami Thakura, Srila Bhaktivinoda Thakura and Srila Narottama Das Thakura, are all pure devotees.

In this book, there is a brief biography of our *guru-varga* which will inspire us to follow the pure devotional path and gradually enable us to establish the loving mission of Lord Chaitanya in the heart of all institutions stemming from Srila Prabhupada's Gaudiya Math. In this age of deception, Lord Chaitanya's mission will establish eternal peace within us ourselves, the present society, as well as the entire universe. Lord Chaitanya's loving mission is to chant the Hare Krishna *maha-mantra* and give due respect to all, being completely free from material recognition, distinction and desire.

Spontaneous love will appear by the grace of the pure devotees of Sri Sri Radha-Krishna and deliver us from the turbulence of this miserable mundane world and the distress that we experience, thus bringing us to pure divine love and eternal bliss.

MANDALA

PO Box 3088
San Rafael, CA 94912
www.mandalaearth.com
info@mandala.org

Find us on Facebook: www.facebook.com/mandalaearth
Follow us on Twitter: @mandalaearth

Library of Congress Cataloging-in-Publication Data available.

ISBN: 978-1-64722-909-2

Readers interested in the subject matter should visit the Gopinath
Gaudiya Math website at www.gopinathgaudiyamath.com or visit one
of the locations below:

Ishodyan, Sri Mayapur, District Nadia, West Bengal, India, 741313

(Old Dauji temple) Gopeswar Road, Vrindavan, Mathura (U.P) India,
281121

Chakratirtha Road, Puri, Orissa, India, 752002

Mandala Publishing, in association with Roots of Peace, will plant
two trees for each tree used in the manufacturing of this book. Roots
of Peace is an internationally renowned humanitarian organization
dedicated to eradicating land mines worldwide and converting war-torn
lands into productive farms and wildlife habitats. Roots of Peace will
plant two million fruit and nut trees in Afghanistan and provide farmers
there with the skills and support necessary for sustainable land use.

Printed in India